CONGREGATION FC

DIRECTORY
MINISTRY AND LIFE
OF PRIESTS

*All documents are published thanks to the generous support
of the members of the Catholic Truth Society*

CATHOLIC TRUTH SOCIETY
PUBLISHERS TO THE HOLY SEE

CONTENTS

INTRODUCTION

The rich experience of the Church concerning the ministry and life of priests, condensed in various documents of the Magisterium,[1] has received in our days a new impulse thanks to the teachings contained in the post-synodal Apostolic Exhortation *Pastores dabo vobis.*

The publication of this document, in which the Supreme Pontiff has wanted to unite his voice as the Bishop of Rome and Successor of Peter to that of the synodal Fathers,[2] represents for priests and for the entire Church, the beginning of a faithful and fruitful way of deepening and applying its contents.

"Today, in particular, the pressing pastoral task of the new evangelisation calls for the involvement of the entire People of God and requires new fervour, new methods and a new expression for the proclaiming and witnessing of the Gospel. This task demands priests who are deeply and fully immersed in the mystery of Christ and capable of embodying a new style of pastoral life".[3]

Those primarily responsible for this new evangelisation of the third Millennium are the priests, who, however, in order to realise their mission, need to nourish in themselves a life which is a pure reflection of their identity, and to live a union of love with Jesus Christ Eternal High Priest, Head and Master, Spouse, and Pastor of his Church. They should strengthen their own spirituality and ministry with a continuous and complete formation.

---

[1] Among the most recent documents, cf. ECUMENICAL. COUNCIL VATICAN II, Dogmatic Constitution on the Church *Lumen gentium* 28; Decree on Priestly Formation *Optatam Totius* 22; Decree on the pastorale Office of the Bishops *Christus Dominus* 16; Decree on the Ministry and life of Priests *Presbyterorum Ordinis;* PAUL VI, Encyclical Letter *Sacerdotalis coelibatus* (24th June 1967): *AAS* 59 (1967), 657-697;S. CONGREGATION FOR THE CLERGY, Circular letter *Inter ea* (4th November 1969): *AAS* 62(1970), 123-134; SYNOD OF BISHOPS, Document on the Ministerial Priesthood *Ultimis temporibus* (30th November 1971): *AAS* 63 (1971), 898-922; *Codex Iuris Canonici* can. 273-289;232-264;1008-1054; CONGREGATION FOR CATHOLIC EDUCATION, *Ratio Fundamentalis Institutiones Sacerdotalis* (19th March 1985), 101; JOHN PAUL II, *Letters* to all the Priests of the Church on Holy Thursday; *Catechesi* on Priests, in the General Audiences from 31st March to 22nd September 1993.

[2] JOHN PAUL II, Post-Synodal Apostolic Exhortation *Pastores dabo vobis* (25th March 1992): *AAS* 84(1992), 657-804.

[3] *Ibid.*, 18: *l.c.*, 685.

This Directory, requested by numerous Bishops during the Synod of 1990 and in a general consultation of the Episcopate promoted by our Congregation, was conceived in order to respond to these needs.

In order to outline the content, the suggestions of the entire world episcopate – consulted on purpose –, the results of plenary sessions of the Congregation held in the Vatican in October of 1993, as well as the considerations of many theologians, and experts on the matter from diverse geographical areas and involved in current pastoral work were taken into account.

Effort was made to offer practical elements for employing initiatives in the most unitary way possible, while avoiding specific conditions which are proper to a particular Diocese or Episcopal Conference. With this in mind, it appeared proper that this Directory recall only those doctrinal elements which are the basis of the identity, spirituality and continuous formation of priests.

The document, therefore, does not intend to offer an exhaustive exposition on the priesthood, nor a mere repetition of what has already been authentically declared by the Magisterium of the Church, but rather to respond to the principal questions of a doctrinal, disciplinary and pastoral nature, placed upon the priests by the demands of the new evangelisation.

Thus, for example, there was a need to clarify the true priestly identity, as the divine Master has willed and as the Church has always seen; it is not reconcilable with those tendencies which would like to empty or annul the reality of the ministerial priesthood. Particular emphasis was given to the theme of communion, a demand especially felt today, with its imminent presence in the life of the priest. The same can be said of priestly spirituality which, in our times, has suffered many contradictions, above all, due to secularism and an erroneous anthropologism. Therefore, it is necessary to offer some counsels for an adequate and permanent formation which may help the priests joyfully and responsibly live their vocation.

The text is directed of course, through the Bishops, to all the priests of the Church of the Latin Rite. The directives contained here concern, in particular, the secular diocesan clergy, although with due adaptations, they can also help priests of religious institutes and of societies of apostolic life.

It is hoped that this Directory be a help for every priest in deepening his identity and in growing in his spirituality; an encouragement in the ministry and permanent formation – for which each one is primarily responsible –, and a point of reference for a rich and authentic apostolate for the good of the Church and of the entire world. From the Congregation for the Clergy, Holy Thursday 1994.

JOSÉ Card. SANCHEZ
Prefect
✠ CRESCENZIO SEPE
Titular Archbishop of Grado
Secretary

CHAPTER I

THE IDENTITY OF THE PRIEST

1. Priesthood as a gift

The entire Church participates in the priestly anointing of Christ in the Holy Spirit. In the Church, in fact, "all the faithful form a holy and royal priesthood, offer spiritual sacrifices through Jesus Christ and proclaim the greatness of him who has called you out of darkness into his marvellous light" (cf. 1 *Pt* 2:5. 9).[4] In Christ, his entire Mystical body is united to the Father through the Holy Spirit for the salvation of all men.

However, the Church cannot carry out this mission alone: all of her work intrinsically needs communion with Christ, the Head of his Body. Indissolubly united to her Lord, she continuously receives from him the effects of grace and truth, of guidance and support so that she may be for all and for each one "a sign and instrument, that is, of communion with God and of unity among all men".[5] The ministerial priesthood finds its reason for being in light of this vital and operative union of the Church with Christ. As a result, through this ministry the Lord continues to accomplish among his People the work which as Head of his Body belongs to him alone. Thus, the ministerial priesthood renders tangible the actual work of Christ, the Head, and gives witness to the fact that Christ has not separated himself from his Church; rather he continues to vivify her through his everlasting priesthood. For this reason, the Church considers the ministerial priesthood a gift given to Her through the ministry of some of her faithful.

This gift which was instituted by Christ to continue his own salvific mission was conferred upon the Apostles and remains in the Church through the Bishops and their successors.

2. Sacramental Roots

Through the sacramental ordination conferred by the imposition of hands and the consecratory prayers of the Bishop, "a specific ontological

---

[4]   ECUMENICAL COUNCIL VATICAN II, Decree *Presbyterorum Ordinis,* 2.

[5]   ECUMENICAL COUNCIL VATICAN II, Dogm. Const. *Lumen gentium,* 1.

bond which unites the priest to Christ, High Priest and Good Shepherd"[6] is established.

Thus, the identity of the priest comes from the specific participation in the Priesthood of Christ, in which the one ordained becomes, in the Church and for the Church, a real, living and faithful image of Christ the Priest, "a sacramental representation of Christ, Head and Shepherd".[7] Through consecration, the priest "receives a spiritual 'power' as a gift which is a participation in the authority with which Jesus Christ, through his Spirit, guides the Church".[8] This sacramental identification with the Eternal High Priest specifically inserts the priest into the trinitarian mystery and, through the mystery of Christ, into the ministerial Communion of the Church so as to serve the People of God.[9]

3. In Communion with the Father, the Son and the Holy Spirit

If it is true that each Christian, by means of Baptism, is in communion with God, One and Triune, it is equally true that by the power of the consecration received with the Sacrament of Holy Orders, the priest is placed in a particular and specific relation with the Father, with the Son and with the Holy Spirit. In fact, "Our identity has its ultimate source in the charity of the Father. He sent the Son, High Priest and Good Shepherd, and we are united sacramentally with the ministerial priesthood through the action of the Holy Spirit. The life and the ministry of the priest are a continuation of the life and the action of the same Christ. This is our identity, our true dignity, the fountain of our joy, the certainty of our life".[10]

Therefore, the identity, the ministry and the existence of the priest are essentially related to the three divine Persons for priestly service to the Church.

4. In the Trinitarian Dynamics of Salvation

The priest, "as a visible continuation and sacramental sign of Christ

---

[6] JOHN PAUL II, Post-Synodal Apostolic Exhortation *Pastores dabo vobis,* 11: *l.c.,* 675.

[7] *Ibid.,* 15: *l.c.,* 680.

[8] Ibid., 21: *l.c.,* 688; cf. ECUMENICAL COUNCIL VATICAN II, Decree *Presbyterorum ordinis,* 2; 12.

[9] CF JOHN PAUL II, Post-Synodal Apostolic Exhortation *Pastores dabo vobis,* 12c: *l.c.,* 676.

[10] *Ibid.,* 18, *l.c.,* 685-686; *Message of the Synod Fathers to the People of God* (28th October 1990), III: "L'Osservatore Romano", 29th-30th October 1990.

in his own position before the Church and the world, as the enduring and ever-new source of salvation",[11] finds himself inserted into the trinitarian dynamics with a particular responsibility. His identity springs from the *ministerium verbi et sacra-mentorum*, which is in essential relation to the mystery of salvific love of the Father (cf. *Jn* 17:6-9. 24; 1 *Co* 1:1; 2 *Co* 1:1), to the priestly being of Christ, who personally chooses and calls his ministers to be with him (cf. *Mk* 3:15), and to the gift of the Spirit (cf. *Jn* 20:21), who communicates to the priest the necessary power for giving life to a multitude of sons of God, united in the one ecclesial body and oriented towards the Kingdom of the Father.

5. Intimate Relation with the Trinity

From this, one perceives the essentially 'relational' characteristic (*Jn* 17:11, 21)[12] Of the priest's identity.

The grace and the indelible character conferred with the sacramental unction of the Holy Spirit,[13] place the priest in personal relation with the Trinity since it is the fountain of the priestly being and work. Therefore, the priest must live this relationship in an intimate and personal manner, in a dialogue of adoration and of love with the three divine Persons, conscious that he has received this gift for the service of all.

Christological Dimension

6. Specific Identity

The Christological dimension, like the Trinitarian dimension, springs directly from the sacrament which ontologically configures the priest to Christ the Priest, Master, Sanctifier and Pastor of his People.[14] The faithful who, maintaining their common priesthood, are chosen and become part of the ministerial priesthood are granted an indelible participation in the one and only priesthood of Christ. This is a participation in the

---

[11] JOHN PAUL II, Post-Synodal Apostolic Exhortation *Pastores dabo vobis,* 16: *l.c.,* 682.

[12] Cf. *ibid.,* 12: *l.c.,* 675-677.

[13] Cf. COUNCIL ECUMENICAL TRIDENTINE, SESSIO XXIII, *Desacramento Ordinis*: DS, 1763-1778; JOHN PAUL II, Post-Synodal Apostolic Exhortation *Pastores dabo Vobis,* 11-18: *l.c.,* 673-686} Catechesi in the general audience of 31st March 1993: "L'Osservatore Romano", 1st April 1993.

[14] Cf. ECUMENICAL COUNCIL VATICAN II, Dogm. Const. *Lumen gentium,* 18-31; Decree *Presbyterorum ordinis,* 2; *C.I.C.,* can. 1008.

public dimension of mediation and authority regarding the sanctification, teaching and guidance of all the People of God. On the one hand, the common priesthood of the faithful and the ministerial or hierarchical priesthood are necessarily ordered one for the other because each in its own way participates in the only priesthood of Christ and, on the other hand, they are essentially different.[15]

In this sense the identity of the priest is new with respect to that of all Christians who through Baptism participate as a whole in the only priesthood of Christ and are called to give witness to Christ throughout the earth.[16] The specificity of the ministerial priesthood lies in the need that the faithful have of the mediation and dominion of Christ which is made visible by the work of the ministerial priesthood.

In this unique identity with Christ, the priest must be conscious that his life is a mystery totally grafted onto the mystery of Christ and of the Church in a new and specific way and that this engages him totally in pastoral activity and rewards him.[17]

7. In the Heart of the People of God

Christ associates the Apostles to his own mission. "As the Father has sent me, I also send you" (*Jn* 20:21). In Holy Ordination itself, the missionary dimension is ontologically present. The priest was chosen, consecrated and sent to carry out effectively in our time this eternal mission of Christ; he becomes his authentic representative and messenger: "He that hears you, hears me; he that despises you, despises me; and he that despises me, despises him that sent me" (*Lk* 10:16)

One can therefore say that the configuration to Christ, through sacramental consecration, defines the role of the priest in the heart of the People of God, making him participate in his own way in the sanctifying, magisterial and pastoral authority of Jesus Christ himself, Head and

---

[15] Cf. ECUMENICAL COUNCIL VATICAN II, Dogm. Const. *Lumen gentium*, 10; Decree *Presbyterorum Ordinis*, 2.

[16] Cf. ECUMENICAL COUNCIL VATICAN II, Decree A*postolicam actuositatem,* 3; JOHN PAUL II, Post-Synodal Apostolic Exhortation *Christifidelis laici* (30th December 1988), 14: *AAS* 81 (1989), 409-413.

[17] Cf. JOHN PAUL II, Post-Synodal Apostolic Exhortation *Pastores dabo vobis*, 13-14:l.c., 677-679; *Catechetics* general audience of 31st March 1993: "L'Osservatore Romano", 1st April, 1993.

Pastor of the Church.[18]

Acting *in persona Christi capitis*, the priest becomes the minister of the essential salvific actions, transmits the truths necessary for salvation and cares for the People of God, leading them towards sanctity.[19]

Pneumatological Dimension

8. Sacramental Character

In priestly Ordination, the priest has received the seal of the Holy Spirit which has marked him by the sacramental character in order to always be the minister of Christ and the Church. Assured of the promise that the Consoler will abide "with him forever" (*Jn* 14:16-17), the priest knows that he will never lose the presence and the effective power of the Holy Spirit in order to exercise his ministry and live with charity his pastoral office as a total gift of self for the salvation of his own brothers.

9. Personal Communion with the Holy Spirit

It is also the Holy Spirit who by Ordination confers on the priest the prophetic task of announcing and explaining, with authority, the Word of God. Inserted in the communion of the Church with the entire priestly order, the priest will be guided by the Holy Spirit whom the Father has sent through Christ. The Holy Spirit teaches him everything and reminds him all Jesus has said to the Apostles. Therefore, the priest with the help of the Holy Spirit and the study of the Word of God in the Scriptures, with the light of Tradition and of the Magisterium,[20] discovers the richness of the Word to be proclaimed to the ecclesial community entrusted to him.

10. Invocation of the Holy Spirit

Through the sacramental character and the identification of his intention with that of the Church, the priest is always in communion with the Holy Spirit in the celebration of the liturgy, especially in the Holy Eucharist and the other sacraments.

In fact, in each sacrament, Christ invoked by the priest who celebrates

---

[18] Cf. JOHN PAUL II, Post-Synodal Apostolic Exhortation *Pastores dabo vobis*, 18: *l.c.*, 684-686.

[19] Cf. *ibid.*, 15: l.c., 679-681.

[20] Cf. ECUMENICAL COUNCIL VATICAN II, Dogm. Const. *Dei Verbum*, 10; Decree *Presbyterorum Ordinis*, 4.

in persona Christi acts through the Holy Spirit with his efficacious power on behalf of the Church.[21]

Thus, the sacramental celebration finds its efficacy in the Word of Christ who has instituted it and in the power of the Holy Spirit which the Church invokes frequently in the epiclesis.

This is particularly evident in the Eucharistic Prayer in which the priest, invoking the power of the Holy Spirit on the bread and on the wine, pronounces the words of Jesus and actualises the mystery of the Body and of the Blood of Christ, really present through transubstantiation.

11. Strength to Guide the Community

It is thus in the communion with the Holy Spirit that the priest finds the strength to guide the community entrusted to him and to maintain it in the unity wanted by the Lord.[22] The prayer of the priest in the Holy Spirit can be patterned on the priestly prayer of Jesus Christ (*Jn* 17). Therefore, he must pray for the unity of the faithful so that they may be one in order that the world may believe that the Father has sent the Son for the salvation of all.

Ecclesial Dimension

12. 'In' and 'in front of the Church'

Christ, the permanent and always new origin of salvation, is the mysterial font from which is derived the mystery of the Church, his Body and his Bride, called by his Spouse to be a sign and instrument of redemption.

Through the mystery of Christ, the priest lives his multiple ministries and is inserted also into the mystery of Church which "becomes aware in faith that her being comes not from herself but from the grace of Christ in the Holy Spirit".[23] In this sense, while the priest is in the Church, he is also set *in front of* it.[24]

13. A Certain Participation in the Spousal Nature of Christ

The Sacrament of Holy Orders, in fact, makes the priest a sharer not only

---

[21] Cf. ECUMENICAL COUNCIL VATICAN II, Decree *Presbyterorum Ordinis*, 5; *Catechism of the Catholic Church*, n. 1120.

[22] Cf. ECUMENICAL COUNCIL VATICAN II, Decree *Presbyterorum Ordinis*, 6.

[23] Cf. JOHN PAUL II, Post-Synodal Apostolic Exhortation *Pastores dabo vobis* 16: *l.c.*, 681.

[24] Cf. *ibid.*

in the mystery of Christ the Priest, Master, Head and Shepherd but, in some way, also in Christ "Servant and Spouse of the Church".[25] This is the 'Body' of him who has loved and loves to the point of giving himself for her (cf. *Ep* 5:25); who renews her and purifies her continually by means of the Word of God and of the sacraments (cf. *Ibid.* 5:26); who works to make her always more beautiful (cf. *Ibid.* 5:27), and lastly, who nourishes her and treats her with care (cf. *Ibid.* 5:29).

The priests, as collaborators of the Episcopal Order, form with their Bishop a sole Presbyterate[26] and participate, in a subordinate degree, in the only priesthood of Christ. Similar to the Bishop, they participate in that spousal dimension in relation to the Church which is well expressed in the Rite of the episcopal ordination when the ring is entrusted to them.[27]

The priest, who "in the individual local communities of the faithful makes the Bishop present, so to speak, to whom they are united with a faithful and great spirit"[28] must be faithful to the Bride and almost like living icons of Christ the Spouse render fruitful the multi-form donation of Christ to his Church.

By this communion with Christ the Spouse, the ministerial priesthood is also founded – as Christ, with Christ and in Christ – in that mystery of transcendent supernatural love of which the marriage among Christians is an image and a participation.

Called to the act of supernatural love, absolutely gratuitous, the priest should love the Church as Christ has loved her, consecrating to her all his energies and giving himself with pastoral charity in a continuous act of generosity.

14. Universality of the Priesthood

The command of the Lord: go to all the nations (*Mt* 28:18-20) definitively expresses the place of the priest *in front of* the Church.[29] Sent, – *missus*

---

25 *Ibid.* 3: l.c. 661.

26 Cf. ECUMENICAL COUNCIL VATICAN II, Dogm. Const. *Lumen gentium* 28; *Decree Presbyterorum Ordinis* 7; Decree *Christus Dominus* 28; Decree *Ad gentes* 19; JOHN PAUL II, Post-Synodal Apostolic Exhortation *Pastores dabo vobis* 17: *l.c.*, 683.

27 Cf. ECUMENICAL COUNCIL VATICAN II, Dogm. Const. *Lumen gentium* 28; *Pontificale Romanum Ordinatio Episcoporum Presbyterorum et diaconorum* cap. I, n. 51, Ed. typica altera, 1990, P. 26.

28 ECUMENICAL COUNCIL VATICAN II, Dogm. Const. *Lumen gentium* 28.

29 Cf. JOHN PAUL II, Post-Synodal Apostolic Exhortation *Pastores dabo vobis* 16: *l.c.*, 681.

– by the Father by means of Christ, the priest pertains "in an immediate way" to the universal Church,[30] which has the mission to announce the Good News unto the "ends of the earth" (*Ac* 1:8).[31]

"The spiritual gift received by priests in Ordination prepares them for a wide and universal mission of salvation".[32] In fact, through Orders and the ministry received, all priests are associated with the Episcopal Body and, in hierarchical communion with it, according to their vocation and grace, they serve the good of the entire Church.[33] Therefore, the membership to a particular Church, through incardination,[34] must not enclose the priest in a restricted and particularistic mentality, but rather should open him to the service of other Churches, because each Church is the particular realisation of the only Church of Jesus Christ, such that the universal Church lives and fulfills her mission in and from the particular Churches in effective communion with her. Thus, all the priests, must have a missionary heart and mind and be open to the needs of the Church and of the world.[35]

15. Missionary Nature of the Priesthood

It is important that the priest be fully aware and profoundly live this missionary reality of his priesthood, in total harmony with the Church who feels the need to send her ministers to places where their mission is more needed and to work toward a more equal distribution of clergy.[36]

---

[30] CONGREGATION FOR THE DOCTRINE OF THE FAITH, Letter on the Church Understood as Communion *Communionis notio* (28th May 1992), 10: *AAS* 85 (1993) 844.

[31] Cf. JOHN PAUL II, Encyclical Letter *Redemptoris Missio* 23a: *AAS* 83 (1991), 269.

[32] ECUMENICAL COUNCIL VATICAN II, Decree *Presbyterorum Ordinis* 10; cf. JOHN PAUL II, Post-Synodal Apostolic Exhortation *Pastores dabo vobis* 32: *l.c.*, 709-710.

[33] Cf. ECUMENICAL COUNCIL VATICAN II, Dogm. Const. *Lumen gentium* 28; Decree *Presbyterorum Ordinis* 7.

[34] Cf. *C.I.C.* can. 266, § 1.

[35] Cf. ECUMENICAL COUNCIL VATICAN II, Dogm. Const. *Lumen gentium* 23; 26; S. CONGREGATION FOR THE CLERGY, Directive Notes Postquam Apostoli (25th March 1980), 5; 14; 23: *AAS* 72 (1980) 346-347; 353-354; 360-361; TERTULLIAN, *De praescriptione* 20, 5-9: *CCL* 1 201-202.

[36] Cf. ECUMENICAL COUNCIL VATICAN II, Dogm. Const. *Lumen gentium* 23; Decree *Presbyterorum Ordinis* 10; JOHN PAUL II, Post-Synodal Apostolic Exhortation *Pastores dabo vobis* 32: *l.c.*, 709-710; S. CONGREGATION FOR THE CLERGY, Directive Notes *Postquam Apostoli* (25th March 1980): *AAS* 72 (1980) 343-364; CONGREGATION FOR THE EVANGELISATION OF PEOPLES *Pastoral Guide for Diocesan Priests that Depend on the Congregation for the Evangelisation of Peoples* (1st October 1989), 4; *C.I.C.* can. 271.

This demand in the life of the Church in the world must be felt and lived by each priest, above all and essentially as the gift of living within the institution and being at her service.

Therefore, we cannot accept those opinions which arise from a misunderstanding of particular cultures, that tend to distort the missionary action of the Church, called to fulfill the same universal mystery of salvation which transcends all cultures and should vivify them.[37]

It must be said that the universal expansion of the priestly ministry today is related to the social-cultural features of the contemporary world in which the need to eliminate all the barriers which divide people and nations is felt and which, especially, through cultural exchange, wants to bind people, despite the geographical distances separating them.

Consequently, today more than ever, the clergy must feel itself apostolically bound to unite all men in Christ and in his Church.

16. Authority as 'amoris officium'

Another sign of the priest placing himself *in front of* the Church is his being a guide who works toward the sanctification of the faithful entrusted to his ministry, which is essentially pastoral.

This reality, which has to be lived with humility and coherence, can be subject to two opposite temptations.

The first is that of exercising his ministry in an overbearing manner (cf. *Lk* 22:24-27; 1 *Pt* 5:1-4), while the second is that of disdaining the configuration to Christ Head and Shepherd because of an incorrect view of community.

The first temptation was also strong for the disciples themselves and was promptly and repeatedly corrected by Jesus; all authority is exercised in the spirit of service, as *amoris officium*[38] and as an unselfish dedication for the good of the flock (cf. *Jn* 13:14; 10:11).

The priest must always remember that the Lord and Master "did not come to be served but to serve" (*Mk* 10:45); he has bent down to wash the feet of the disciples (cf. *Jn* 13:5) before dying on the Cross and before sending them out to the whole world (cf. *Jn* 20:21).

---

[37] Cf. CONGREGATION FOR THE EVANGELISATION OF PEOPLES, *Pastoral Guide for Diocesan Priests that Depend on the Congregation for the Evangelisation of Peoples* (1st October 1989); JOHN PAUL II, Encyclical Letter *Redemptoris Missio* (7th December 1990), 54; 67: *AAS* 83 (1991), 301-302; 315-316.

[38] Cf. ST. AUGUSTINE, *In Iohannis Evangelium Tractatus* 123, 5: CCL 36, 678.

The priests will give authentic testimony to the Resurrected Lord, to whom was given "all power in heaven and on earth" (cf. *Mt* 28:18), if they exercise their own power in a humble, authoritative service to his own flock[39] and with respect to the duties which Christ and the Church entrusted to the lay faithful[40] and to the consecrated faithful for the profession of the evangelical counsels.[41]

17. Temptation of 'Democratism'

It often happens that to avoid this first deviation, one falls into the second, eliminating all the differences in the roles among the members of the Mystical Body of Christ, which is the Church. This practically negates the true doctrine of the distinction between the common and ministerial priesthood.[42]

One of the dangers noticeable today is the so-called 'democratism'. In respect to this, it should be remembered that the Church recognises all the merits and values which the democratic culture has brought to human society. At the same time, the Church has always fought with all the means within its reach for the recognition of the equal dignity among all men.

With this strong ecclesial tradition the Vatican Council II openly spoke about the dignity of all the baptised in the Church.[43]

Nevertheless, it is still necessary to affirm that the mentality and current practice in cultural and social-political trends of our times cannot be transferred automatically to the Church. The Church, indeed, owes its existence and structure to the salvific plan of God. She sees herself as a *gift* from the benevolence of a Father who has saved her through the humiliation of his Son on the cross. Therefore, the Church, through the Holy Spirit, wants to be completely consonant and faithful to the free and liberating

---

[39] Cf. JOHN PAUL II, Post-Synodal Apostolic Exhortation *Pastores dabo vobis* 21: *l.c.,* 688-690; *C.I.C.*, can. 274.

[40] Cf. *C.I.C.*, cann. 275, § 2; 529, § 1.

[41] Cf. *ibid.*, can. 574, § 1.

[42] Cf. COUNCIL ECUMENICAL TRIDENTINE, Sessio XXIII, *De Sacramento Ordinis* cap. 1 e 4, cann. 3, 4, 6: DS 1763-1776; ECUMENTICAL COUNCIL VATICAN II, Dogm. Const. *Lumen gentium* 10; S. CONGREGATION FOR THE DOCTRINE OF THE FAITH, Letter to the Bishops of the Catholic Church on Certain Questions Concerning the Minister of the Eucharist *Sacerdotium ministeriale* (6th August 1983), 1: *AAS* 75 (1983), 1001.

[43] Cf. ECUMENICAL VATICAN COUNCIL II, Dogmatic Constitution *Lumen gentium* 9.

will of its Lord Jesus Christ. This mystery of salvation makes the Church by its specific nature, into a reality diverse from the simple human society.

Hence, the so-called 'democratism' becomes a grave temptation because it leads to a denial of the authority and capital grace of Christ and to distort the nature of the Church; it would be almost just a human society. Such a view damages the very hierarchical structure willed by its Divine Founder as the Magisterium has always clearly taught and the Church herself has lived from the start.

The participation in the Church is based upon the mystery of communion which, by its nature, sees in itself the presence and action of the ecclesiastical hierarchy.

Therefore, the mentality which confuses the duties of the priests with those of the lay faithful cannot be permitted in the Church. It is sometimes manifested in some ecclesial organisations of participation. In like manner, it does not distinguish the proper authority of the Bishop from that of the priests as collaborators of the Bishops, or denies the Petrine primacy in the College of Bishops.

To this effect, it should be remembered that the presbyterate and the Council of Priests are not an expression of the right of association of the clergy, and even less can be understood according to views of a syndicalistic nature which claim interests of parties foreign to the ecclesial community.[44]

18. Distinction between Common an Ministerial Priesthood

The distinction between the common and ministerial priesthood, far from creating division among the members of the Christian community, harmonises and unifies the life of the Church. This, in fact, as regards the Body of Christ, is an organic communion among all the members, in which each one serves the community by fulfilling his own distinct role and specific vocation (1 *Co* 12:12 ff.).[45]

Therefore, no one may licitly change what Christ has wanted for his Church. It is indissolubly linked with its Founder and Head who alone may provide her, through the power of the Holy Spirit, with ministers in the service of the faithful.

---

[44] Cf. ECUMENICAL VATICAN COUNCIL II, *Presbyterorum Ordinis*, 7.

[45] Cf. CONGREGATION FOR THE EVANGELISATION OF PEOPLES, *Pastoral Guide for Diocesan Priests that Depend on the Congregation for the Evangelisation of Peoples* (1st October 1989), 3.

No community can take the place of Christ, who is the one who calls, consecrates and sends forth ministers, through the legitimate Pastors even in a situation of particular necessity, when it might consider granting itself its own priest, in ways contrary to the dispositions of the Church.[46] The solution to these cases of necessity is Jesus' prayer: "pray therefore the Lord of the harvest, that he send forth labourers into his harvest" (*Mt* 9:38). If to this prayer done with faith, the fervent life of charity of the community is added, we can be sure that the Lord will not fail to give pastors according to his heart (cf. *Jr* 3:15).[47]

19. Only the Priests are Pastors

One way to avoid falling into this 'democratistic' mentality is to shun the so-called "clericalisation" of the laity,[48] which tends to diminish the ministerial priesthood of the priest. After the Bishop, the term 'pastor' can only be attributed in a proper and univocal sense to the priest by virtue of the ministerial priesthood received with the Ordination. The attribute 'pastoral', in fact, refers both to the *potestas docendi et sanctificandi*, and to the *potestas regendi*.[49]

It should be remembered that these tendencies do not favour the true advancement of the laity because they frequently forget the authentic ecclesial vocation and mission of the laity in the world.

Priestly Communion

20. Communion with the Trinity and with Christ

In light of the above-mentioned regarding the priest's identity, the communion of the priest is fulfilled above all with the Father, the ultimate origin of all his power; with the Son, in whose redemptive mission he

---

[46] Cf. S. CONGREGATION FOR THE DOCTRINE OF THE FAITH, Letter to the Bishops Of the Catholic Church on some questions regarding the minister Of the Eucharist *Sacerdotium ministeriale* (6th August 1983), II. 3, III. 2: *AAS* 75 (1983), 1001-1009; *Catechism of the Catholic Church* n. 875.

[47] Cf. ECUMENICAL VATICAN COUNCIL II, Decree *Presbyterorum Ordinis*, 11.

[48] Cf. JOHN PAUL II, *Address* to the Episcopate of Switzerland (15th July, 1984): *Insegnamenti*, VII/1 (1984), 1784.

[49] Cf. JOHN PAUL II *Address* to the participants of the International Symposium on "The Priest Today": "L'Osservatore Romano", 29th May, 1993; Address to the participants of the International symposium "Ius in vita et in missione Ecclesiae" (23rd April, 1993), in "L'Osservatore Romano", 25th April, 1993.

participates; with the Holy Spirit, who gives him the power for living and fulfilling that pastoral charity which qualifies him in a priestly way.

In fact, "the nature and the mission of the ministerial priesthood cannot be defined except in this multiple and rich network of relations which spring from the Blessed Trinity and is prolonged in the communion of the Church as a sign, in Christ, of the union with God and the unity of the whole human race".[50]

21. Communion with the Church

The priest's communion-relation with the Church in its aspect of mystery and ecclesial community comes from this fundamental union-communion with Christ and the Trinity.[51] In fact, it is within the mystery of the Church, as a mystery of trinitarian communion with a missionary zeal that the identity of every Christian is revealed and, therefore, the specific and personal identity of the priest and of his ministry as well.

Precisely, the ecclesial communion of the priest is lived in diverse ways. In fact, through sacramental Ordination, he develops special bonds with *the Pope, the Episcopal Body, his own Bishop, other priests and the lay faithful.*

22. Hierarchical Communion

Communion as a characteristic of the priest-hood is based on the unity of the Head, Shepherd and Spouse of the Church, who is Christ.[52]

In such ministerial communion some precise ties are shaped with the Pope, the College of Bishops and each one's diocesan Bishop. "There can be no genuine priestly ministry except in communion with the Supreme Pontiff and the Episcopal College, especially with one's own diocesan Bishop, who deserves that filial respect and obedience promised during the rite of ordination".[53] Thus, this refers to a hierarchical communion, that is to say, a communion in that hierarchy in the same way that it is structured within.

This communion, in virtue of participation subordinated to the

---

[50] JOHN PAUL II, Post-Synodal Apostolic Exhortation *Pastores dabo vobis*, 12: *l.c.,* 676; cf. ECUMENICAL COUNCIL VATICAN II, Dogm. Const. *Lumen gentium,* 1.

[51] Cf. ECUMENICAL VATICAN COUNCIL II Dogmatic Constitution *Lumen gentium*, 8.

[52] Cf. ST AUGUSTINE, *Sermo* 46, 30: *CCL* 41, 555-557.

[53] JEAN PAUL II, Post-synodal Apostolic Exhortation *pastures dabo vobis*, 28: *l.c.,* 701-702.

Bishops in the one ministerial priesthood and mission, also involves the spiritual and organic-structural bond of priests with the entire Episcopal order, their own Bishop,[54] the Roman Pontiff as Pastor of the universal Church[55] and each particular Church. This is strengthened by the fact that the entire Episcopal order as a whole and each Bishop individually must be in hierarchical communion with the Head of the College.[56] This College, in fact, is composed only of those consecrated Bishops who are in hierarchical communion with its Head and members.

23. Communion in the Eucharistic Celebration

Hierarchical communion is vividly expressed in the Eucharistic prayers; when the priest prays for the Pope, the College of Bishops and his own Bishop, he not only expresses a sentiment of devotion, but attests to the authenticity of his celebration as well.[57]

The Eucharistic concelebration itself, in the circumstances and conditions foreseen,[58] especially when presided by the Bishop and with the participation of the faithful, manifests well the unity of the priesthood of Christ in his ministers, as well as the unity of the sacrifice of the People of God.[59] Moreover, it contributes to the consolidation of sacramental fraternity which exists among priests.[60]

---

[54] Cf. ECUMENICAL COUNCIL VATICAN II, Cost. dogm. *Lumen gentium* 28; Decree *Presbyterorum Ordinis* 7; 15.

[55] Cf. *C.I.C.* cann. 331; 333 § 1

[56] Cf. ECUMENICAL COUNCIL VATICAN II, Dogm. Const. *Lumen gentium* 22; Decree *Christus Dominus* 4; *C.I.C.* can. 336.

[57] Cf. S. CONGREGATION FOR THE DOCTRINE OF THE FAITH, Letter on the Church Understood as Communion *Communionis notio* (28th May 1992), 14: *AAS* 85 (1993), 847.

[58] Cf. C.I.C. can. 902; SACRED CONGREGATION FOR THE SACRAMENTS AND DIVINE LITURGY, Decree *Promulgato Codice* (12th September, 1983), II, I, 153: *Notitiae* 19 (1983), 542.

[59] Cf. ST. THOMAS OF AQUINAS, *Summa Theol.* q. 82, a. 2 ad 2, *Sent.* IV d. 13, q. 1, a. 2, q. 2; ECUMENICAL COUNCIL VATICAN II, Const. *Sacrosanctum Concilium*, 41, 57; S. CONGREGATION OF RITES, General Decree *Ecclesiae semper* (7th March, 1965): AAS 57 (1965), 410-412; Instruction *Eucharisticum Mysterium* (25th May, 1965), 47: *AAS* 57 (1967), 565-566.

[60] Cf. S. CONGREGATION OF RITES, Instruction *Eucharisticum Mysterium* (25th May, 1967), 47: *AAS* 59 (1967), 565-566.

24. Communion in the Ministerial Activity

Each priest should have a deep, humble and filial bond of charity with the person of the Holy Father and adhere to his petrine ministry of magisterium, of sanctification and of government, with exemplary docility.[61]

In his fidelity and service to the authority of his Bishop, he lives the communion called for by the practice of his priestly ministry. For the pastors with more experience it is easy to confirm the need to avoid any form of subjectivism in his ministry and adhere with responsibility to pastoral programs. Besides being an expression of maturity, such adhesion contributes to the building of that unity in the communion which is indispensable for the work of evangelisation.[62]

With full respect for hierarchical subordination, the priest will promote a genuine rapport with his Bishop, indicated by sincere confidence, cordial friendship, and true effort towards consonance and convergence in ideals and programs. Nothing should take away from the intelligent capacity for personal initiative and pastoral enterprise.[63]

25. Communion in the Priesthood

By virtue of the Sacrament of Holy Orders "every priest is united to the other members of the priesthood by specific bonds of apostolic charity, ministry and fraternity".[64] He is, in fact inserted into the *Ordo Presbyterorum* constituting that unity which can be defined as a true family in which the ties do not come from flesh nor from blood but from the grace of Holy Orders.[65]

---

[61] Cf. *C.I.C.* can. 273.

[62] Cf. ECUMENICAL COUNCIL VATICAN II, Decree *Presbyterorum Ordinis* 15; JOHN PAUL II, Post-Synodal Apostolic Exhortation *Pastores dabo vobis* 65; 79: *l.c.*, 770-772; 796-798.

[63] SAINT IGNATIUS OF ANTIOCH, *Ad Ephesios* XX 1-2: "...If the Lord will reveal to me that, each one on his own and everyone together... you are united in heart through an unshakeable submission to the Bishop and the presbyterate, breaking the only bread which is remedy of immortality, an antidote to prevent death, and to live forever in Jesus Christ": *Patres Apostolici* ed. F.X. FUNK, II 203-205.

[64] JOHN PAUL II, Post-Synodal Apostolic Exhortation *Pastores dabo vobis* 17: l.c. 683; cf. ECUMENICAL COUNCIL VATICAN II, Dogm. Const. *Lumen gentium* 28; Decree *Presbyterorum Ordinis* 8; *C.I.C.*, can. 275 § 1.

[65] Cf. JOHN PAUL II, Post-Synodal Apostolic Exhortation *Pastores dabo vobis*, 74: *l.c.*, 790; CONGREGATION FOR THE EVANGELISATION OF THE PEOPLES, *Pastoral Guide for Diocesan Priests that Depend on the Congregation for the Evangelisation of Peoples* (1st October, 1989),6.

This membership in a specific presbyterate,[66] always comes within the context of a particular Church, of an Ordinariate or of a personal Prelature. In fact, unlike the case of the College of Bishops, it seems that there are no theological foundations to affirm the existence of a universal Presbyterate.

Priestly fraternity and membership to a presbyterate are, therefore, elements characterising the priest. The rite of the imposition of the hands by the Bishop and all of the priests present during the priestly Ordination has special significance and merit because it points to the equality of participation in the ministry, and to the fact that the priest cannot act by himself; he acts within the presbyterate becoming a brother of all those who constitute it.[67]

26. Incardination in Particular Church

Incardination in a particular Church[68] constitutes an authentic juridical bond[69] which also has a spiritual value, since from it springs "the rapport with the Bishop in the sole presbyterate, sharing in the ecclesial solicitude, in dedication to the evangelical care of the People of God in specific historical conditions and settings".[70] In this perspective, the bond with the particular Church is rich in meaning for pastoral action as well.

It should not be forgotten that the secular priests not incardinated in the Diocese and the priest members of a religious institute or of a society of apostolic life who live in the Diocese[71] and exercise some office therein,[72] although still placed under their legitimate Ordinaries, belong by full or a diverse title to the clergy of such Diocese[73] where "they have the right to both an active and a passive voice in an election to the council of

---

[66] Cf. ECUMENICAL COUNCIL VATICAN II, Decree *Presbyterorum Ordinis* 8; *C.I.C.* cann. 369, 498, 499.

[67] Cf. *Pontificale Romanum De Ordinatione Episcopi Presbyterorum et Diaconorum* chapter II, nn. 105; 130, editio typica altera, 1990, PP. 54; 66-67; ECUMENICAL COUNCIL VATICAN II, Decree *Presbyterorum Ordinis* 8.

[68] Cf. *C.I.C.*, can. 265.

[69] Cf. JOHN PAUL II, *Address* in the cathedral of Quito to Bishops, Priests, Religious and Seminarians (29th January, 1985): *Insegnamenti* VII/1(1985), 247-253.

[70] JOHN PAUL II Post-Synodal Apostolic Exhortation *Pastores dabo vobis* 31: *l.c.*, 708.

[71] Cf. *ibid.* 17;74; *l.c.*, 683;790.

[72] *C.I.C.* can. 498 §1,2.

[73] JOHN PAUL II Post-Synodal Apostolic Exhortation *Pastores dabo vobis* 31: *l.c.* 708-709.

priests".[74] The religious priests, in particular, by unity of powers, share the pastoral care offering the contribution of specific charisma and "with their presence inspiring the particular Church to live more vividly its universal openness".[75]

The priests, then, incardinated in a Diocese, who are serving an ecclesial movement approved by the competent ecclesiastical Authority,[76] are aware of being members of the presbyterate of their Diocese and must sincerely collaborate with it. The Bishop of incardination, on his part, must respect the way of life required by the membership to a Movement, and it may be fitting, by the norm of the law, to permit the priest to lend his services to other churches, if this forms part of the charisma of the movement itself.[77]

27. The Presbyterate: a Place of Sanctification.

The presbyterate is a privileged place in which the priest should be able to find the means of sanctification and evangelisation and of being helped to overcome the limits and the weaknesses which are proper to human nature and which are particularly felt today.

He will therefore make every effort to avoid living his own priesthood in an isolated and subjectivistic way, and must try to enhance fraternal communion in the giving and receiving – from priest to priest – of the warmth of friendship, of affectionate help, of acceptance, of fraternal correction, well aware that the grace of Orders "assumes and elevates human relations, psychologically, affectionately, cordially and spiritually".[78]

All this is expressed in the liturgy of the Mass *In Coena Domini* of Holy Thursday which shows how through Eucharistic communion – born in the Last Supper – the priests receive the capacity to love one another, as the Master loves them.[79]

---

[74] Cf. *ibid* 31;41;68: *l.c.*, 708;728-729;775-777.

[75] Cf. *C.I.C.* can. 271.

[76] JOHN PAUL II Post-Synodal Apostolic Exhortation *Pastores dabo vobis* 74: *l.c.*, 790.

[77] JOHN PAUL II, *Catechesi* in the General Audience of 4th August 1993, n.4: "L'Osservatore Romano", 5th August 1993.

[78] Cf. ECUMENICAL COUNCIL VATICAN II, Decree *Presbyterorum Ordinis* 12-14.

[79] Cf. *ibid* 8.

28. Priestly Friendship

The profound ecclesial sense of the presbyterate fosters the personal responsibility of each priest in carrying out the particular ministry entrusted to him by the Bishop.[80] The capacity to develop and profoundly live priestly friendship is a source of serenity and joy in the exercise of the ministry, a decisive support in difficulties and a valuable help in the growth of pastoral charity. Priests must exercise this friendship in a particular way precisely towards those brothers most in need of understanding, help and support.[81]

29. Common Life

A manifestation of this communion is also the *common life* always supported by the Church, recently emphasised by the documents of Vatican Council II [82] and of the successive Magisterium,[83] and applied in many Dioceses with positive results.

Among the diverse forms of this (communal house, community of table, etc.) one must look highly upon the communal participation in liturgical prayer.[84] The diversity of forms must be encouraged according to the possibilities and practical situations, without necessarily emphasising models proper to religious life. Particularly praiseworthy are those associations which support priestly fraternity, sanctity in the exercise of the ministry, and communion with the Bishop and with the entire Church.[85]

It is necessary that parish priests be available to encourage common life in the parochial house pastoral care. with their vicars,[86] effectively considering them as their cooperators and sharers of the pastoral care.

---

[80] Cf. ST AUGUSTINE, *Sermones* 355, 356, *De vita et moribus clericorum: PL* 39, 1568-1581.

[81] Cf. ECUMENICAL COUNCIL VATICAN II, Cost. dogm. *Lumen gentium* 28c; Decree *Presbyterorum Ordinis* 8; Decree *Christus Dominus* 30a.

[82] Cf. SACRED CONGREGATION OF BISHOPS, DIRECTORY *Ecclesiae Imago* (22nd February 1973), n. 112: *C.I.C.* cann. 280; 245, § 2; 550, § 1; JOHN PAUL II, Post-Synodal Apostolic Exhortation *Pastores dabo vobis* 81: *l.c.*, 799-800.

[83] Cf. ECUMENICAL COUNCIL VATICAN II, Cost. *Sacrosanctum Concilium* 26; 99; *Liturgia Horarum Institutio Generalis* n. 25.

[84] Cf. *C.I.C.* can. 278, 5 2; JOHN PAUL II Post-Synodal Apostolic Exhortation *Pastores dabo vobis* 31; 68; 81: *l.c.,* 708; 777; 799.

[85] Cf. *C.I.C.* can 550 § 2.

[86] Cf. *ibid,* can. 545 § 1.

And the vicars, in order to build priestly communion, must recognise and respect the authority of the parish priest.[87]

30. Communion with the Lay Faithful

As a man of communion, the priest cannot express his love for the Lord and for the Church without transmitting it in a real and unconditional love for all Christians, the object of his pastoral care.[88]

Like Christ, he must make Christ "visible in the midst of the flock" entrusted to his care,[89] having a positive and encouraging rapport with the lay faithful. Recognising in these their dignity as sons of God, he develops his own role in the Church, and in their service he offers all his priestly ministry and pastoral charity.[90] In the awareness of the profound communion which binds him to the lay faithful and to the religious, the priest will make every effort "to awaken and deepen co-responsibility in the one common mission of salvation, with a prompt and heartfelt esteem for all the charisma and tasks which the Spirit gives believers for the building up of the Church".[91]

More specifically, the parish priest, in his continuous concern for the common good in the Church, will encourage associations of the faithful and movements,[92] embracing them all, and helping them to find among themselves a unity of goals, prayer and apostolic action.

Insofar as he unites the family of God and brings about the Church as communion, the priest becomes the bridge between man and God, making himself a brother of men who wants to be their pastor, father and master.[93] The priest will guide the man of today, in his search for the meaning of

---

[87] Cf. JOHN PAUL II, Catechesi in the General Audience of 7th July 1993: "L'Osservatore Romano", 8th July 1993; ECUMENICAL COUNCIL VATICAN II, Decree *Presbyterorum Ordinis* 15b

[88] JOHN PAUL II, Post-Synodal Apostolic Exhortation *Pastores dabo vobis*, 15: *l.c.*, 679-680.

[89] Cf. ECUMENICAL COUNCIL VATICAN II, Decree *Presbyterorum Ordinis*, 9; *C.I.C.*, cann. 275 § 2; 529 § 2.

[90] JOHN PAUL II Post-Synodal Apostolica Exhortation *Pastores dabo vobis*, 74: *l.c.*, 788.

[91] Cf. *C.I.C.*, can. 529 § 2.

[92] Cf. JOHN PAUL II, Post-Synodal Apostolic Exhortation *Pastores dabo vobis*, 74: *l.c.*, 788; PAUL VI, Encyclical Letter *Ecclesiam suam* (6th August 1964), III: *AAS* 56 (1964), 647.

[93] Cf. JOHN PAUL II, *Catechesi* in the General Audience of 7th July "L'Osservatore Romano", 8th July 1993.

his existence, to a personal encounter with Christ, an encounter which is realised as a message and as a reality already present, although not in a definitive way, in the Church. In such a way the priest, placed in the service of the People of God, will present himself as an expert in humanity, a man of truth and of communion, a witness of the solicitude of the Only Shepherd for each and every member of his flock. The community will be able to count on his dedication, availability, untiring work of evangelisation and, above all, his devoted and unconditional love.

Therefore, he will exercise his spiritual mission with kindness and firmness, with humility and service,[94] opening himself to compassion, participating in the sufferings which arise from the various forms of poverty, spiritual and material, old and new. He will know also how to act with humility and with mercy within the difficult and uncertain ways of the conversion of sinners, to which he will exercise the gift of truth and patience and the encouraging benevolence of the Good Shepherd, who does not reprove the lost sheep, but carries it on his shoulders and celebrates for its return to the fold (cf. *Lk* 15:4-7).[95]

31. The Communion with Religious Members of Institutes of Consecrated Life

Particular attention will be reserved to relations with the brothers and the sisters engaged in a life of special consecration to God in all their forms, showing them a sincere appreciation and a real spirit of apostolic collaboration, respecting and promoting their specific charisma. He will co-operate, moreover, so that the consecrated life always appears more luminous for the benefit of the entire Church and more persuasive and attractive to the new generations.

In such spirit of esteem for the consecrated life, the priest will give particular care to those communities which, for various reasons, are greatly in need of good doctrine, of assistance and of encouragement in the faith.

32. Pastoral Works and Vocations

In his pastoral work, each priest will take particular care concerning vocations, encouraging prayer for vocations, doing his best in the work

---

[94] Cf. *C.I.C.*, can. 529 § 1.

[95] Cf. ECUMENICAL VATICAN COUNCIL II, Decree *Presbyterorum Ordinis* 11; *C.I.C.* can. 233 § 1.

of catechetics, and taking care of the formation of the ministers. He will promote appropriate initiatives through a personal rapport with those under his care, allowing him to discover their talents and to single out the will of God for them, permitting a courageous choice in following Christ.[96]

Above all, a clear knowledge of one's specific identity, a unity of life, a transparent cheerfulness, and a missionary zeal are the indispensable elements of the vocational work that must be an integral and organic part of ordinary pastoral action.

The priest will always maintain relations of cordial collaboration and of sincere affection with the seminary, for it is the cradle of his vocation and the first place in which he experienced communal life.

It would be desirable that every priest be concerned with inspiring at least one priestly vocation which could thus continue the ministry.

33. Political and Social Obligation

The priest, as servant of the universal Church, cannot tie himself to any historical contingency, and therefore must be above any political party. He cannot take an active role in political parties or labour unions, unless, according to the judgement of the ecclesiastical authority, the rights of the Church and the defence of common good require it.[97] In fact, even if these are good things in themselves, they are nevertheless foreign to the clerical state since they can constitute a grave danger of division in the ecclesial communion.[98]

Like Jesus (cf. *Jn* 6:15 ff.), the priest "ought to refrain from actively engaging himself in politics, as it often happens, in order to be a central point of spiritual fraternity".[99] All the faithful, therefore, must always be able to approach the priest without feeling inhibited for any reason.

---

[96] JOHN PAUL II Post-Synodal Apostolic Exhortation *Pastores dabo vobis* 74c: *l.c.*, 789.

[97] Cf. *C.I.C.*, can. 287 § 2; SACRED CONGREGATION FOR THE CLERGY, Decree *Quidam Episcopi* (8th March 1982), *AAS* 74 (1982), 642-645.

[98] Cf. CONGREGATION FOR THE EVANGELISATION OF THE PEOPLES, *Pastoral Guide for Diocesan Priests that Depend on the Congregation for the Evangelisation of Peoples* (1st October 1989), 9 SACRED CONGREGATION FOR THE CLERGY, Decree *Quidam Episcopi* (8th March 1982), *AAS* 74 (1982), 642-645.

[99] JOHN PAUL II Catechism of the General Audience of 28th July 1993 n. 3: "L'Osservatore Romano", 29th July 1993, cf. ECUMENICAL COUNCIL VATICAN II Pastoral Constitution *Qaudium et Spes*, 43; SYNOD OF BISHOPS, Document on Ministerial Priesthood *Ultimis temporibus* (30th November 1971), II, I, 2b: *AAS* 63 (1971), 912-913 *C.I.C.*, cann. 285 § 3; 287 § 1

The priest will remember that "it does not fall on the shoulders of the Pastors of the Church to intervene directly in political activities and in social organisations. This task, in fact, forms part of the lay faithful vocation, in which they work by their own initiative together with their fellow citizens".[100] Nevertheless, he will not be absent "in the effort to form in them an upright conscience".[101]

The reduction of his mission to temporal tasks, of a purely social or political nature, is foreign to his ministry, and does not constitute a triumph but rather a grave loss to the Church's evangelical fruitfulness.

---

[100] *Catechism of the Catholic Church*, n. 2442; cf. *C.I.C.*, can. 227.

[101] SYNOD OF BISHOPS, Document on Ministerial; Priesthood *Ultimis temporibus* (30th November 1971), II, I, 2b: *AAS* 63 (1971), 913.

CHAPTER II

PRIESTLY SPIRITUALITY

Current Historical Context

34. Interpreting the Signs of the Times

The life and ministry of priests always develop within a particular historical context, at times replete with new problems and unforeseen changes, in which the pilgrim Church lives.

The priesthood is not born of history, but of the immutable will of God. However, it corresponds with historical circumstances and, to remain always faithful to its nature, is configured, in specific choices, through a critical relation and a demand of evangelical harmony with the 'sign of the times'. Therefore, priests have the duty to interpret these 'signs' in the light of faith and subject them to prudent judgement. In any case, they cannot ignore them, especially if they wish to effectively orient their own lives in a way that will make their service and testimony more fruitful for the kingdom of God.

In the current era of the life of the Church and society, priests are called to live their ministry with depth, anticipating the ever more profound, numerous and sensitive demands not only of a pastoral nature, but also social and cultural, which they must face.[102]

Today these priests, therefore, are engaged in diverse areas of apostolate which require complete dedication and generosity, intellectual preparation and, above all, a mature and deep spiritual life rooted in pastoral charity, which is their specific way to holiness and which also constitutes an authentic service to the faithful through pastoral ministry.

35. The Demands of the New Evangelisation

Thus it is clear that the priest is involved in a very special way in the effort of the entire Church to carry out the new evangelisation. Based on faith in Jesus Christ, Redeemer of mankind, the priest is assured that in him rests

---

[102] Cf. JOHN PAUL II, Post-Synodal Apostolic Exhortation *Pastores dabo vobis*, 5: *l.c.*, 663-665.

an "unfathomable richness" (*Ep* 3:8) which no culture nor era can exhaust which men can always draw on for their enrichment.[103]

This is a time therefore for a renewal of our faith in Jesus Christ, who is the same "yesterday, today and for ever" (*Heb* 13:8). Therefore "the call to the new evangelisation is above all a call to conversion".[104] At the same time, it is a call to that hope, "which rests upon the promises of God, on the fidelity to his Word, and which has the *resurrection of Christ* as an unshakeable certainty, his definitive victory over sin and death, the first announcement and root of every evangelisation, foundation of every human advancement, the starting point of every authentic Christian culture".[105]

In this context, the priest must above all revive his faith, his hope and his sincere love for the Lord, in such a way as to be able to present him for the contemplation of the faithful and all men as he truly is: a living and fascinating Person, who loves us more than anyone else because he has given his life for us; "greater love has no man than this, that a man give his life for his friends" (*Jn* 15:13).

At the same time, the priest, conscious that each person is, in diverse ways, looking for a love that is capable of bringing them beyond the anguishes concomitant with human weakness and egoism, and above all with death itself, must proclaim that Jesus Christ is the answer to all these anxieties.

In the new evangelisation, the priest is called to be the *herald of hope*.[106]

36. The Challenge of Sects and New Cults

The proliferation of sects and new cults, as well as their diffusion also among the Catholic faithful, constitutes a particular challenge to the pastoral ministry. At the root of these phenomena lie complex causes. At all events, the priestly ministry is called to respond promptly and incisively to the search for the sacred and for authentic spirituality which today is emerging in a particular way.

In recent years, in effect, it has become evident that there is an eminently pastoral necessity for the priest to be a man of God and a teacher of prayer.

---

[103] Cf. JOHN PAUL II, Inaugural Address to the IV General Conference of Latin American Bishops (Santo Domingo, 12th-28th October 1992), n. 24: *AAS* 85 (1993), 826.

[104] *Ibid.*, 1: *l.c.*, 808-809.

[105] *Ibid.* 25: *l.c.* 827

[106] Cf. *ibid.*

At the same time, this obliges the priest to be welcoming towards the community entrusted to his pastoral care in such a way that no member of the community would be made to feel anonymous or think themselves an object of indifference.

This is a responsibility which indeed falls on all the faithful, but in a special way on the priest, who is the man who brings about communion.

If he knows how to receive each one who approaches him with esteem and respect, appreciative of their value as persons, then he will generate an authentic charity which will become contagious and will gradually extend itself through the entire community.

To rise to the challenge of sects and new cults, a mature and comprehensive catechesis is of particular importance. This, at the present time, requires that the priest make a special effort to ensure that his faithful really understand the meaning of their Christian vocation and of their Catholic faith. The faithful must be educated, in a particular way, to understand well the relationship between their specific vocation in Christ and their belonging to his Church which must learn to love in a filial and tenacious way.

This will all come to pass if the priest, in his life and in his ministry, avoids everything which could either be the cause of timidity or coldness towards, or restrict the identification with the Church.

37. Lights and Shadows in Ministerial Activity

It is greatly comforting to note that today priests of all ages and in the great majority carry out their ministry with joyful effort, often the result of silent heroism, working with all their strength without seeing at times, the fruits of their labour.

Through this effort, today they form a living expression of that divine grace which, given freely in the moment of Ordination, continues to grant an ever-renewing strength to their ministry.

Along with this light, there is no lack of shadows which tend to weaken its beauty and render as less credible their testimony to the world.

Pastoral ministry is a fascinating undertaking, yet arduous, open to misunderstanding and marginalisation, and, especially today, to fatigue, challenge, isolation and, at times, solitude.

To rise to the challenge continuously presented him by the secularist mentality, the priest must make every effort to protect the absolute primacy of his spiritual life, his continuous presence with Christ and his generous pastoral charity, intensifying his communion with all men and, above all, with other priests.

Being with Christ in Prayer

38. Priority of Spiritual Life

The priesthood was, so to speak, *conceived* in that long prayer during which our Lord Jesus spoke with the Father about his Apostles and, certainly, all those who in the course of time, would be made participants in his very mission (cf. *Lk* 6:12; cf. *Jn* 17:15-20). The very prayer of Jesus in Gethsemane (cf. *Mt* 26:36-44), leading toward the priestly sacrifice of Golgotha, manifests in a paradigmatic way "how our priesthood should be profoundly linked to prayer: rooted in prayer".[107]

Born of these prayers and called to renew a Sacrifice inseparable from these, priests maintain their ministry with a spiritual life to which they give absolute pre-eminence, avoiding any neglect due to other activities. Precisely in order to effectively carry out his pastoral ministry, the priest must enter into a special and profound rapport with Christ the Good Shepherd, who alone remains the principal protagonist in any pastoral action.

39. Means for the Spiritual Life

Such a spiritual life must be embodied in each priest through the liturgy, personal prayer, his lifestyle and the practice of the Christian virtues, which contribute to the richness of ministerial action. The very conformity to Christ requires one to breathe, so to speak, in a climate of friendship and personal encounter with the Lord and in service to the Church, his Body, for which the priest will show his love through the faithful fulfilment and defence of the duties of pastoral ministry.[108]

It is necessary, therefore, that the priest programme his life of prayer in a manner which embraces: the daily Eucharistic celebration,[109] with

---

[107] JOHN PAUL II, *Letter* to Priests on Holy Thursday (13th April 1987), 10: *AAS* 79 (1987) 1292.

[108] Cf. *C.I.C.*, can. 276 § 2, 1.

[109] Cf. ECUMENICAL COUNCIL VATICAN II, Decree *Presbyterorum Ordinis* 5;18; JOHN PAUL II, Post-Synodal Apostolic Exhortation *Pastores dabo vobis* 23; 26; 38; 46; 48: *l.c.*, 691-694; 697-700; 720-723; 738-740; 742-745; *C.I.C.* cann. 246, § 1; 276 5 2, 2.

adequate preparation and thanksgiving; frequent confession[110] and spiritual direction already practised in the seminary;[111] the complete and fervent celebration of the liturgy of the hours,[112] on a daily basis;[113] examination of conscience;[114] mental prayer;[115] divine readings;[116] the prolonged moments of silence and prayer, above all in periodical Spiritual Exercises and Retreats;[117] the affectionate expression of Marian devotions, like the Rosary;[118] the *Via Crucis* and other pious exercises;[119] and the fruitful reading on lives of the saints.[120]

Each year during the Mass of Holy Thursday, as a sign of enduring desire of fidelity, priests renew in the presence of the Bishop, and together with him, the promises made in the moment of Ordination.[121]

---

[110] Cf. ECUMENICAL COUNCIL VATICAN II, *Decree Presbyterorum Ordinis* 5;18; *C.I.C.* cann. 246 § 4; 276 § 2, 5; JOHN PAUL II Post-Synodal Apostolic Exhortation *Pastores dabo Vobis*, 26;48: *l.c.*, 697-700, 742-745.

[111] Cf. ECUMENICAL COUNCIL VATICAN II, Decree *Presbyterorum Ordinis* 18; *C.I.C.* can. 239; JOHN PAUL II Post-Synodal Apostolic Exhortation *Pastores dabo vobis*, 40;50; 81: *l.c.*, 724-726; 746-748; 799-800.

[112] Cf. ECUMENICAL COUNCIL VATICAN II, Decree *Presbyterorum Ordinis* 18; *C.I.C.* cann. 246 § 2; 276 § 2, 3; JOHN PAUL II, Post-Synodal Apostolic Exhortation *Pastores dabo vobis* 26; 72: *l.c.*, 697-700; 783-797.

[113] Cf. *C.I.C.*, can. 1174 § 1.

[114] ECUMENICAL COUNCIL VATICAN II, Decree *Presbyterorum Ordinis* 18; JOHN PAUL II, Post-Synodal Apostolic Exhortation *Pastores dabo vobis* 26; 37-38; 47; 51; 53; 72: *l.c.*, 697-700; 718-723, 740-742, 748-750, 751-753-783-787

[115] Cf. *C.I.C.* can. 276 § 2, 5.

[116] Cf. ECUMENICAL COUNCIL VATICAN II, Decree *Presbyterorum Ordinis* 4; 13; 18; JOHN PAUL II Post-Synodal Apostolic Exhortation *Pastores dabo vobis* 26; 47; 53; 70; 72: *l.c.*, 697-700; 740-742; 751-753; 778-782; 783-787.

[117] Cf. ECUMENICAL COUNCIL VATICAN II, Decree *Presbyterorum Ordinis* 18; *C.I.C.* can. 276 § 2, 4; JOHN PAUL II Post-Synodal Apostolic Exhortation *Pastores dabo vobis*, 80: *l.c.* 798-800.

[118] Cf. ECUMENICAL COUNCIL VATICAN II, Decree *Presbyterorum Ordinis* 18; *C.I.C.* cann. 246 § 3; 276 § 2, 5. JOHN PAUL II, Post-Synodal Apostolic Exhortation *Pastores dabo vobis*, 36;38;45;82: *l.c.*, 715-718; 720-723; 736-738; 800-804.

[119] Cf. ECUMENICAL COUNCIL VATICAN II, Decree *Presbyterorum Ordinis* 18; JOHN PAUL II, Post-Synodal Apostolic Exhortation *Pastores dabo vobis* 26; 37-38; 47; 51; 53; 72: *l.c.*, 697-700; 718-723-740-742, 748-750, 751-753, 783-787

[120] Cf. ECUMENICAL COUNCIL VATICAN II, Decree *Presbyterorum Ordinis* 18c.

[121] JOHN PAUL II Letter to Priests for Holy Thursday 1979 *Novo incipiente* (8th April 1979), 1: *AAS* 71(1979), 394; Post-Synodal Apostolic Exhortation *Pastores dabo vobis* 80: *l.c.*, 798-799.

The care for the spiritual life should be felt as a joyful duty on the part of the priest himself, and also as a right of the faithful who seek in him, consciously or not, the *man of God*, the counsellor, the mediator of peace, the faithful and prudent friend, the sure guide to confide in during the more difficult moments in life to find encouragement and security.[122]

40. Imitating Christ in Prayer

Due to numerous duties stemming in large part from pastoral activity, the priest's life is linked, now more than ever, to a series of requests which could lead to a growing *exterior activism*, submitting that life to a frenetic and disordered pace.

In light of such a 'temptation', one must not forget that the initial intention of Jesus in convoking the Apostles around him was above all that they "remain with him" (*Mk* 3:14).

The Son of God himself has wished to leave us a testimony of his prayer.

In fact, the Gospels frequently present us with Christ in prayer: in the revelation of his mission by the Father (cf. *Lk* 3:21-22), before the calling of the Apostles (cf. *Lk* 6:12), in giving thanks to God in the multiplication of the bread (cf. *Mt* 14:19; 15:36; *Mk* 6:41; 8:7; *Lk* 9:16; *Jn* 6:11), in the Transfiguration (cf. *Lk* 9:28-29), the healing of the deaf-mute (cf. *Mk* 7:34) and raising of Lazarus (cf. *Jn* 11:41 ff.), before the confession of Peter (cf. *Lk* 9:18), when he teaches the disciples how to pray (cf. *Lk* 11:1), and when these return after completing their mission (cf. *Mt* 11:25 ff.; *Lk* 10:21 ff.), in the blessing of the children (cf. *Mt* 19:13) and in the prayer for Peter (cf. *Lk* 22:32).

All of his daily life is rooted in prayer. Thus, he retreated to the desert or the mountain to pray (cf. *Mk* 1:35; 6:46; *Lk* 5:16; *Mt* 4:1; *Mt* 14:23), rose early (cf. *Mk* 1:35) and spent the entire night in prayer to God (cf. *Mt* 14:23-25; *Mk* 6:46-48; *Lk* 6:12).

Near the end of his life, at the Last Supper (cf. *Jn* 17:1-26), in the agony of the garden (cf. *Mt* 26:36-44) and on the Cross (cf. *Lk* 23:34-46; *Mt* 27:46; *Mk* 15:34), the divine Master demonstrated that prayer gave life to his Messianic ministry and to his paschal exodus. Risen from the dead, he lives forever and prays for us (cf. *Heb* 7:25).[123]

Following the example of Christ, the priest must know how to maintain

---

[122] Cf. POSSIDIO, *Vita Sancti Aurelii Augustini* 31: PL 32, 63-66

[123] Cf. *Liturgia Horarum, Institutio generalis*, nn. 3-4.

the vivacity and abundance of the moments of silence and prayer in which he cultivates and deepens his own essential relationship with the living figure of Jesus Christ.

41. Imitating the Church in Prayer

To remain faithful to the obligation of 'being with Christ', it is necessary that the priest know how to imitate the Church in prayer.

In giving the Word of God, which he himself has received with joy, the priest is reminded of the exhortation given by the Bishop on the day of his Ordination: "Therefore, making the Word the object of your continual reflection, always believe what you read, teach what you believe, carry out in your life what you teach. In this way, through the doctrine which nourishes the People of God and with life's upright testimony which comforts and sustains them, you will become a builder of the temple of God, which is the Church". Likewise regarding the celebration of the sacraments, and in particular the Eucharist: "Be aware, then, of what you are doing, understand what is being fulfilled and why you are celebrating the mystery of the death and Resurrection of the Lord, bear the death of Christ in your body and walk in the newness of life". And, finally, regarding the pastoral guidance of the People of God so as to lead them to the Father: "Therefore, never turn your face from Christ, the Good Shepherd, who has come not to be served, but to serve, and to seek and save those who are lost".[124]

42. Prayer as Communion

Strengthened by the special bond with the Lord, the priest will know how to confront those moments in which he could feel alone among men; effectively renewing his being with Christ who in the Eucharist is his refuge and best repose.

Like Christ, who was often alone with the Father (cf. *Lk* 3:21; *Mk* 1:35), the priest also must be the man who finds communion with God in

---

[124] *Pontificale Romanum – Deordinatione Episcopi, Presbyterorum et Diaconorum*, cap. II, n. 151, Ed. typica altera 1990, pp. 87-88.

solitude,[125] so he can say with St Ambrose: "I am never less alone than as when I am alone".[126]

Beside the Lord, the priest will find the strength and the means to bring men back to God, to enlighten their faith, to inspire commitment and sharing.

Pastoral Charity

43. Manifestation of the Charity of Christ

Pastoral charity constitutes the internal and dynamic principle capable of uniting the multiple and diverse pastoral activities of the priest and, given the social-cultural and religious context in which he lives, is an indispensable instrument for drawing men to a life in Grace.

Informed by such charity, the ministerial activity must be a manifestation of the charity of Christ. With this charity the priest will demonstrate in his bearing and conduct the total self-giving of himself to the flock with which he has been entrusted.127

Assimilating the pastoral charity of Christ in such a way as to make it part of his own life is a goal which requires continuous effort and sacrifice by the priest, since this charity cannot be improvised, nor considered acquired or attained definitively. The minister of Christ must feel obliged to live and give testimony to this reality always and everywhere, even when, due to his age, he be relieved of his specific pastoral assignments.

44. Functionalism

Pastoral charity faces the danger, today especially, of being emptied of its meaning through so-called 'functionalism'. It is not rare, in fact, to perceive, even in some priests, the influence of an erroneous mentality which reduces the ministerial priesthood to strictly functional aspects. To merely play the role of the priest, carrying out a few services and ensuring completion of various tasks would make up the entire priestly existence.

---

[125] Cf. ECUMENICAL COUNCIL VATICAN II, Decree *Presbyterorum Ordinis*, 18; SYNOD OF BISHOPS, Document on Ministerial Priesthood *Ultimis temporibus* (30th November 1971), II, 1, 3: *AAS* 63 (1971), 913-915; JOHN PAUL II, Post-Synodal Apostolic Exhortation *Pastores dabo vobis*, 46-47: *l.c.*, 738-742; *Catechesi* in the General Audience of 2nd June 1993, n. 3: "L'Osservatore Romano", 3rd June 1993.

[126] "Numquam enim minus solus sum, quam cum solus esse videor": *Epist.* 33 (Maur. 49), *CSEL*, 82, 229.

[127] Cf. ECUMENICAL COUNCIL VATICAN II, Decree *Presbyterorum Ordinis*, 14; JOHN PAUL II, Post-Synodal Apostolic Exhortation *Pastores dabo vobis*, 23: *l.c.*, 691-694.

Such a reductive conception of the identity of the ministry of the priest risks pushing their lives towards an emptiness, an emptiness which often comes to be filled by lifestyles not consonant with their very ministry.

The priest, who knows how to be the minister of Christ and his Spouse, will also find in prayer, in study and in spiritual reading, the strength necessary to over-come these dangers.[128]

Preaching the Word

45. Fidelity to the Word

Christ entrusted to the Apostles and to the Church the mission of preaching the Good News to all men.

To transmit the faith is to reveal, to proclaim and to deepen in the Christian vocation; thus, the calling which God addresses to each man in showing him the mystery of salvation and, likewise, the place which he must hold in reference to that mystery, as an adopted son in the Son.[129] This dual aspect is succinctly brought to light in the Symbol of Faith, one of the most revealing expressions with which the Church has always responded to the call of God.[130]

Seen thus, the priestly ministry is presented with two demands which are virtually the two sides of the same coin. In the first place, there is the missionary character of the transmission of the faith. The ministry of the Word cannot be abstracted or distanced from the life of the people; indeed, it must make direct reference to the meaning of the life of man, of each man, and, therefore, must have a role in the most pressing questions present in the human conscience.

On the other hand there exists a demand of authenticity and of conformity with the faith of the Church, guardian of the truths concerning God and man. So it must be carried out with extreme responsibility, aware that it entails a question of the greatest importance which concerns the life of man and the meaning of his existence.

For an effective ministry of the Word, the priest, aware of this context, will highlight the testimony of life, which reveals the power of the love of

---

[128] Cf. *C.I.C.* can. 279, 5 1.

[129] Cf. ECUMENICAL COUNCIL VATICAN II, Dogm. Const. *Dei Verbum*, 5; *Catechism of the Catholic Church*, 1-2, 142.

[130] Cf. *Catechism of the Catholic Church*, 150-152; 185-187.

God and gives authenticity to his words. Moreover, he will keep in mind the explicit preaching of the mystery of Christ to the faithful, to non-believers and to non-Christians; of the catechism, which is the ordered and organic exposition of the doctrine of the Church; of the application of revealed truth to specific cases.[131]

The awareness of the absolute necessity of being founded on and of 'remaining' faithful to the Word of God and Tradition in order to be true disciples of Christ and to know the truth (cf. *Jn* 8:31-32) has always accompanied the history of priestly spirituality and has also been authoritatively expressed by Vatican Council II.[132]

Above all for contemporary society, marked by theoretical and practical materialism, by subjectivism and scepticism, it is necessary that the Gospel be presented as "the power of God unto salvation to everyone who believes" (*Rm* 1:16). Priests, remembering that "the faith depends on hearing, and on hearing the Word of Christ" (*Rm* 10:17), devote all of their energy to correspond to this mission which is primary in their ministry. These, in fact, are not only witnesses, but also the heralds and transmitters of the faith.[133]

Such ministry, developed within the hierarchical community, enables him to authoritatively express the Catholic faith and give *official* testimony of the faith of the Church. The People of God, in effect, "is formed into one in the first place by the Word of the living God, which is quite rightly sought from the mouth of priests".[134]

In order to be authentic, the Word must be transmitted "without duplicity and without any dishonesty, but rather manifesting with frankness the truth before God" (2 *Co* 4:2). The priest will wisely avoid falsifying, reducing, distorting or diluting the content of the divine message. His role, in fact, "is not to teach his own wisdom but the Word of God and to issue an urgent invitation to all men to conversion and to holiness".[135]

Preaching, therefore, cannot be reduced to the presentation of one's own thought, to the manifestation of personal experience, to simple

---

[131] Cf. JOHN PAUL II *Catechesi* in the General Audience of 21st April 1993, n. 6: "L'Osservatore Romano", 22nd April 1993.

[132] Cf. ECUMENICAL COUNCIL VATICAN II Dogm. Const. *Dei Verbum* 25.

[133] Cf. *C.I.C.* cann. 757, 762, 776.

[134] Cf. ECUMENICAL VATICAN COUNCIL II Decree *Presbyterorum Ordinis* 4.

[135] *Ibid.*; cf. JOHN PAUL II, Post-synodal Apostolic Exhortation *Pastor dabo vobis* 26: *l.c.*, 697-700.

explanations of a psychological,[136] sociological or humanitarian nature; nor can it excessively concentrate on rhetoric, so often found in mass-communication. It concerns proclaiming a Word which cannot be altered, because it has been entrusted to the Church in order to protect, penetrate and faithfully transmit it.[137]

46. Word and Life

The awareness of one's own mission to proclaim the Gospel must always find concrete expression in pastoral activity. Thus the diverse situations and settings in which he carries out his ministry will be vivified in the light of the Word of God.

In order to be effective and credible, the priest, within the perspective of the faith and his ministry, and with a constructively critical outlook, must be familiar with the ideology, language, cultural intricacies and the typologies diffused in the mass media and which, to a large part, conditions the attitudes of society.

Stirred by the Apostle who exclaimed: "Woe to me if I do not preach the Gospel!" (1 Co 9:16), he must know how to use all of those means of communication which modern science and technology provide.

Certainly, not all depends on such means or human capacity, since divine grace can achieve its effects independently of the works of man. However, in the plan of God, the preaching of the Word is, normally, the preferred channel for the transmission of the faith and for the mission of evangelisation.

For all those who today are removed or are far from the message of Christ, the priest will hear the particularly urgent and anguished plea: "How are they to believe him whom they have not heard? And how are they to hear, if no one preaches?" (Rm 10:14).

To respond to such questions, he must feel personally bound to cultivate, in a particular way, a knowledge of Holy Scripture with a sound exegesis, principally patristic, and meditated on according to the various methods supported by the spiritual tradition of the Church, in order to obtain a living understanding of love.[138] Seen in this light, the priest

---

[136] Cf. JOHN PAUL II, *Catechesi* in the General Audience of 21st April 1993: "L'Osservatore Romano", 22nd April 1993.

[137] Cf. JOHN PAUL II, *Catechesi* in the General Audience of 21st April 1993: "L'Osservatore Romano", 22nd April 1993.

[138] Cf. S. THOMAS AQUINAS, *Stumna Theologiae* I q. 43, a. 5.

will feel the duty of paying particular attention to the preparation, be it remote or proximate, of liturgical homilies, to their content, to the balance between the theoretical and practical aspects, to the manner of teaching and to the technique of delivery, even to good diction, respectful of the dignity of the matter and of the listeners.[139]

47. Word and Catechetics

Catechetics plays a prominent role in this mission of evangelisation, being the preferred instrument for the teaching and development of the faith.[140]

The priest, as a collaborator with the Bishop, has received the mandate and responsibility of encouraging, co-ordinating and directing the catechetical activity of the community with which he has been entrusted. He must know how to integrate such activity into an organic project of evangelisation, guaranteeing, above all, the communion of the catechesis of his community with the person of the Bishop, with the particular Church and with the universal Church.

In particular, he must know how to inspire precise and opportune responsibility and in catechesis, be it with members of the Institutes of Consecrated Life and societies of apostolic life, be it with the lay faithful,[141] to be adequately prepared, showing these the recognition and esteem for the catechetical task.

He must put special interest in caring for the initial and permanent formation of catechists, of associations and movements. To the extent possible, the priest must be the *catechist of catechists*, forming in these a veritable community of disciples of the Lord which serves as a point of reference for those receiving instruction.

Master[142] and educator of the faith,[143] the priest will ensure that the catechism, especially where it concerns the sacraments, will be a primary part in the Christian education of the family, in religious instruction, in apostolic formation and movements, etc., and that it be brought to all the faithful: children, adolescents, adults, the elderly. He will, moreover,

---

[139] Cf. *C.I.C.*, can. 769.

[140] Cf. JOHN PAUL II, Apostolic Exhortation *Catechesi Tradendae* (16th October 1979), 18: *AAS* 71 (1979), 1291-1292.

[141] Cf. *C.I.C.*, can. 768.

[142] Cf. *C.I.C.*, can. 776.

[143] Cf. ECUMENICAL COUNCIL VATICAN II, Decree *Presbyterorum Ordinis* 9.

know how to transmit the catechetical teaching using all those means, teaching aids and instruments of communication which can be of use to the faithful, in a manner proper to their character, capacity, age and condition in life, so as to teach them more fully the doctrine of the Church and to how apply it in the most fitting way.[144]

To such end, the priest has the Catechism of the Catholic Church as his principle point of reference. This text, in fact, contains the sound and authentic norm of the teaching of the Church.[145]

The Sacrament of the Eucharist

48. *The Eucharistic Mystery*

If the service of the Word is the foundational element of the priestly ministry, the heart and vital centre of it is constituted, without a doubt, in the Eucharist, which is, above all, the real presence in time of the unique and eternal sacrifice of Christ.[146]

The sacramental memorial of the death and Resurrection of Christ, the true and efficacious representation of the singular redemptive Sacrifice, source and apex of Christian life in the whole of evangelisation,[147] the Eucharist is the beginning, means, and end of the priestly ministry, since "all ecclesiastical ministries and works of the apostolate are bound up with the Eucharist and are directed towards it".[148] Consecrated in order to perpetuate the Holy Sacrifice, the priest thus manifests, in the most evident manner, his identity.

There exists, in fact, an intimate rapport between the centrality of the Eucharist, pastoral charity, and the unity of life of the priest,[149] who finds in this rapport the decisive indications for the way to the holiness to which he has been specifically called.

If the priest lends to Christ, Most Eternal High Priest, his intelligence, will, voice and hands so as to offer, through his very ministry, the sacramental sacrifice of redemption to the Father, he should make his

---

[144] Cf. *ibid.* 6.

[145] Cf. *C.I.C.* can. 779

[146] Cf. JOHN PAUL II, Apostolic Const. *Fidei Depositum* (11th October 1992), 4.

[147] Cf. JOHN PAUL II, *Catechesi* in the General Audience of 12th May 1993, n. 3: "L'Osservatore Romano", 14th May 1993.

[148] Cf. ECUMENICAL COUNCIL VATICAN II, Decree *Presbyterorum Ordinis*, 5.

[149] *Ibid.*

own the dispositions of the Master and, like him, live those *gifts* for his brothers in the faith. He must therefore learn to unite himself intimately to the offering, placing his entire life upon the altar of sacrifice as a revealing sign of the gratuitous and anticipatory love of God.

49. Celebrating the Eucharist Well

It is necessary to recall the irreplaceable value that the daily celebration of the Holy Mass has for the priest,[150] be it in the presence of other faithful or not. He must live it as the central moment of his day and of his daily ministry, fruit of a sincere desire and an occasion for a deep and effective encounter with Christ, and he must take the greatest care to celebrate it with intimate participation of the mind and heart.

In a society ever more sensitive to communication through signs and images, the priest must pay adequate attention to all of that which can enhance the decorum and sacredness of the Eurcharistic celebration. It is important that, in such ceremonies, proper attention is given to the appropriateness and cleanliness of the place, the structure of the altar and tabernacle,[151] the dignity of the sacred vessels, the vestments,[152] the hymns,[153] the music,[154] the necessary silence,[155] etc. These are all elements which can contribute to a better participation in the Eucharistic Sacrifice. In fact, a lack of attention to the symbolic aspects of the liturgy and, even more, carelessness and coldness, superficiality and disorder, empty the meaning and weaken the process of strengthening the faith.[156] Those who improperly celebrate the Mass reveal a weakness in their faith and fail to educate the others in the faith. Celebrating the Eucharist well, however, constitutes a highly important catechesis on the Sacrifice.

The priest, then, in order to place at the service of the Eucharistic celebration all of his gifts and to render it vivifying in the participation of all of the faithful, must follow the rite established in the liturgical

---

[150] Cf. *ibid.* 5; 13; ST JUSTIN, *Apologia* 1 67: *PG* 6, 429-432; ST AGUSTINO, *Inhannis Etvangelium Tractatus* 26, 13-15: *CCL* 36, 266-268.

[151] Cf. *C.I.C.*, can. 904.

[152] Cf. ECUMENICAL COUNCIL VATICAN II, Cost *Sacrosanctum Concilium,* 128.

[153] Cf. *ibid.,* 122-124.

[154] Cf. *ibid.,* 112, 114, 116.

[155] Cf. *ibid.,* 120; *C.I.C.,* can. 932.

[156] Cf. *ibid.,* 30.

books approved by the competent authority, without adding, removing or changing anything.[157]

All Ordinaries, Superiors of Institutes of Consecrated Life, Moderators of societies of apostolic life and all other Prelates have the grave duty, besides that of being the first in example, of watching over the liturgical norms regarding the celebration of the Eucharist, so that they be faithfully observed in all places.

Priests who celebrate and concelebrate are obliged to wear the sacred vestments prescribed by the rubrics.[158]

50. Eucharistic Adoration

The centrality of the Eucharist should be apparent not only in the worthy celebration of the Sacrifice, but also in the proper adoration of the Sacrament, so that the priest might be the model for the faithful also in devote attention and diligent meditation – whenever possible – done in the presence of our Lord in the tabernacle. It is hoped that the priests entrusted with the guidance of communities dedicate long periods of time for communal adoration and reserve the greatest attention and honour for the Most Blessed Sacrament of the altar, also outside of Holy Mass, over any other rite or gesture. "Faith and love for the Eucharist will not allow Christ to remain alone in his presence in the tabernacle".[159]

A special time of Eucharistic adoration could be during the celebration of the Liturgy of the Hours, which constitutes a true prolongation, during the day, of the sacrifice of praise and thanksgiving which has the Holy Mass as its sacramental centre and source. The Liturgy of the Hours, in which the priest, united to Christ, is the voice of the Church throughout the world, will be celebrated, even in community, when this be possible and in a proper way, so as to be "the interpreter and instrument of the universal voice which sings the glory of God and prays for the salvation of man".[160]

---

[157] Cf. *C.I.C.*, can. 899 § 3.

[158] Cf. ECUMENICAL COUNCIL VATICAN II, Cost. *Sacrosanctum Concilium*, 22; *C.I.C.*, can. 846 § 1.

[159] Cf. C.I.C., can. 929; *Missale Romanum, Institutio generalis*, nn. 81; 298; S. CONGREGATION FOR THE DIVINE CULT, Instruction *Litugicae instaurationes* (5th September 1970), 8c: AAS 62 (1970), 701.

[160] JOHN PAUL II *Catechesi* in the General Audience of 9th June 1993, n. 6: "L'Osservatore Romano", 10th June 1993; cf. Post-Synodal Apostolic Exhortation *Pastores dabo vobis* 48: *l.c.*, 744; S. CONGREGATION OF RITES, Instruction *Eucharisticum Mysterium* (25th May 1967), 50: AAS 59 (1967), 539-573; *Catechism of the Catholic Church* 1418.

An exemplary solemnity of this celebration will be reserved to the canonical chapters.

Therefore, whether it be in communal or individual celebration, the Liturgy of the Hours must never be reduced to a mere 'duty' of mechanically performing a simple and lukewarm reading, without the necessary attention to the text's meaning.

The Sacrament of Penance

51. Minister of Reconciliation

The Holy Spirit for the remission of sins is a gift from the Resurrection to the Apostles: "Receive the Holy Spirit; whose sins you shall forgive, they are forgiven them; and whose sins you shall retain, they are retained." (*Jn* 20:21-23). God has exclusively entrusted the work of reconciliation of man with God to his Apostles and to those who succeed them in the same mission. Priests, then, by the will of Christ, are the only ministers of the Sacrament of Reconciliation.[161] Like Christ, they are invited to call sinners to conversion and bring them back to the Father, by means of a merciful judgement.

Sacramental Reconciliation re-establishes friendship with God the Father and with all his sons in his family which is the Church, which, in turn, is rejuvenated and edified in all of its dimensions: universal, diocesan, parochial.[162]

In spite of the reality of a loss of the sense of sin, greatly extended in the culture of our times, the priest must practice, with joy and dedication, the ministry of the formation of consciences, pardon and peace.

It is necessary, therefore, that he know how to identify himself, in a certain sense, with this sacrament, and assuming the disposition of Christ, reach out with mercy, like the good Samaritan, to a wounded humanity, and thus make known the Christian novelty of the redemptive dimension of Penance, with its healing and pardon.[163]

---

[161] JOHN PAUL II *Catechesi* in the General Audience of 2nd June 1993, n. 5: "L'Osservatore Romano", 3rd June 1993, cf. ECUMENICAL COUNCIL VATICAN II, Cost. *Sacrosanctum Concilium* 99-100.

[162] Cf. TRIDENTINE ECUMENICAL COUNCIL, sess. VI, *de iustificatione* c. 14; sess. XIV, *de poenitentia* c. 1 2, 5-7, can. 10; sess. XXIII, *de ordine* c. 1: DS 1542-1543; 1668-1672; 1679-1688; VATICAN ECUMENICAL COUNCIL II, Decree *Presbyterorum Ordinis* 2, 5; *C.I.C.* can. 965.

[163] Cf. *Catechism of the Catholic Church*, n. 1443-1445.

52. Dedication to the Ministry of Reconciliation

Because of his office[164] and because of his sacramental ordination, the priest must dedicate time and energy to hearing the confessions of the faithful,[165] who, as experience shows, come freely to receive this sacrament as long as there are priests available. This goes even more so for churches in more frequented areas and for sanctuaries. Here a fraternal and responsible collaboration with elderly priests and religious is possible.

Every priest must follow the ecclesial norm which defends and promotes the value of individual and personal confession, the upright accusation of sins indirect colloquy with the confessor,[166] reserving the use of general confession and absolution to only extraordinary cases which fulfil the required conditions, in accord with the existing norms.[167] The confessor will have a way of enlightening the conscience of the penitent with words which, however brief, will be appropriate for that particular situation, and thus enhance a renewed personal orientation toward conversion and make a deep impression upon his spiritual journey, also through the imposition of an opportune penance.[168]

In each case, the priest must know how to maintain the celebration of Reconciliation on a sacramental level, overcoming the danger of reducing it to a purely psychological or simply formalistic act.

This will be manifested by, among other things, faithfully following the norms governing the place for hearing confession.[169]

53. The Necessity of Confession

Like any good faithful, the priest also needs to confess his own sins and weaknesses. He is the first to realise that the practice of this sacrament reinforces his faith and charity toward God and his brothers.

In order to effectively reveal the beauty of Penance, it is essential that the minister of the sacrament offer a personal testimony preceding

---

[164] Cf. *C.I.C.*, cann. 966 § 1; 978 5 1; 98i; JOHN PAUL II Discourse to the Apostolic Penitentiary (27th March 1993): "L'Osservatore Romano", 28th March 1993.

[165] Cf. *C.I.C.*, can. 986.

[166] Cf. *ibid.* can. 960; JOHN PAUL II, Encyclical letter *Redemptor hominis* 20: *AAS* 71 (1979), 309-316.

[167] Cf. *C.I.C.* cann. 961-963; PAUL VI Allocution (20th March 1978), *AAS* 70 (1978), 328-332; JOHN PAUL II, Allocution (30th January 1981): *AAS* 73 (1981), 201-204; Post-synodal Apostolic Exhortation Reconctliatio et Paenitentia (2nd December 1984), 33: *AAS* 77 (1985), 269-271.

[168] Cf. *C.I.C.*, cann. 978 § l; 981.

[169] Cf. *ibid.* can. 964

the other faithful in living the experience of pardon. This constitutes the first condition for restoring the pastoral value of the Sacrament of Reconciliation. In this sense, it is good for the faithful to see and know that their priests go to confession regularly:[170] "the entire priestly existence falls into decay if there is lacking, through neglect or for any other motive, the periodic recourse, inspired by true faith and devotion, to the Sacrament of Penance. In a priest who no longer went to confession or did so poorly, his essence and action as priest would feel the effects very quickly, as would the community of which he is pastor".[171]

54. Spiritual Direction for the Priest and for the Others

Along with the Sacrament of Reconciliation, the priest must also exercise the ministry of spiritual direction. The rediscovery and extension of this practice, also in moments outside of the administration of Penance, is greatly beneficial for the Church in these times.[172] The generous and active attitude of priests in practising it also constitutes an important occasion for identifying and sustaining the vocations to the priesthood and to the various forms of consecrated life. In order to contribute to the improvement of their spirituality it is necessary that they themselves practice spiritual direction. By placing the formation of their soul in the hands of a wise fellow-member, they will enlighten the conscience, from the first steps in the ministry, and realise the importance of not walking alone along the paths of spiritual life and pastoral duties. In making use of this efficacious means of formation, so well-founded in the Church, priests will have full freedom in choosing the person who will guide them.

Guide of the Community

55. Priest for the Community

The priest is also called to meet demands, other than those already seen, within another realm of his ministry. These demands concern the caring

---

[170] Cf. *ibid.* can. 276 § 2, 5; ECUMENICAL COUNCIL VATICAN II Decree *Presbyterorum Ordinis* 18b.

[171] JOHN PAUL II, Post-Synodal Apostolic Exhortation *Reconciliatio et Paenitentia* (2nd December 1984), 31: *AAS* 77 (1985), 266; Post-Synodal Apostolic Exhortation *Pastores dabo vobis* 26. *l.c,* 699.

[172] Cf. JOHN PAUL II, Post-Synodal apostolic Exhortation *Reconciliatio et Paenitentia* 32: *AAS* 77 (1985) (2nd December 1984), 267-269.

for the life of the community with which he has been entrusted and which is primarily expressed in his testimony of charity.

As pastor of the community, the priest exists and lives for it; he prays, studies, works and sacrifices himself for the community. He is disposed to give his life for it, loving it as Christ does, pouring out upon it all his love and consideration,[173] lavishing it with all his strength and unlimited time in order to render it, in the image of the Church, Spouse of Christ, always more beautiful and worthy of the benevolence of God and the love of the Holy Spirit.

This spousal dimension of the priest as pastor will help him guide his community in service to each and every one of its members, enlightening their consciences with the light of revealed truth, wisely guarding the evangelical authenticity of the Christian life, correcting errors, forgiving, curing the sick, consoling the afflicted, and promoting fraternity.[174]

This refined and complete attention, will not only guarantee an ever more effective charity, but also will manifest the deep communion which should exist between the priest and his community, which is like an extension of the communion with God, with Christ, and with the Church.[175]

56. In Tune with the Church

In order to be a good guide of his People, the priest must also be attentive to the signs of the times: those larger and deeper ones which concern the universal Church and its sojourn in the history of man, and those which more closely affect the specific situation of a particular community.

This discernment requires the constant and correct study of theological and pastoral problems, and the exercise of a knowledgeable reflection on the social, cultural and scientific data presented to our epoch.

---

[173] Cf. JOHN PAUL II, Post-Synodal Apostolic Exhortation *Pastores dabo vobis*, 22-23: l.c., 690-694; Apostolic Letter *Mulieris dignitatem* (15th August 1988), 26: *AAS* 80 (1988), 1715-1716.

[174] Cf. ECUMENICAL VATICAN COUNCIL II, Decree *Presbyterorum Ordinis*, 6; *C.I.C.*, can. 529 § 1.

[175] ST JOHN CHRYSOSTOM, *De sacerdotio*, III, 6: *PG*, 48, 643-644: "The spiritual birth of the souls is entrusted to priests: they bring souls to the life of grace through baptism; through them we put on Christ, we are buried with the Son of God and we become members of his Body (cf. *Rm* 6:1; *Ga* 3:27). Therefore we should not only respect the priest more than princes and kings, but esteem him more than we do our parents. Indeed, our parents have begotten us through blood and by the will of the flesh (cf. *Jn* 1:13); while the priests have brought us to life as sons of God; they are the instruments of our joyful rebirth, of our freedom and of our adoption in the order of grace".

In carrying out their mission, priests must know how to transfer these demands into a constant and sincere attitude of *being in tune with the Church*, and thus will always work within a bond of communion with the Pope, Bishops, other brothers in the priesthood, as well as with the faithful consecrated through the profession of the evangelical counsels and with the lay faithful.

They, moreover, will not fail to request, in legitimate ways and taking into account the capacity of each one, the co-operation of the consecrated faithful and the lay faithful, in exercising their mission.

Priestly Celibacy

57. Steadfast Will of the Church

Convinced of the profound theological and pastoral motives upholding the relationship between celibacy and the priesthood, and enlightened by the testimony which confirms to this day, in spite of painful negative cases, its spiritual and evangelical validity, the Church has reaffirmed in Vatican Council II and repeatedly in teachings of the Pontifical Magisterium the "firm will to maintain the law which requires celibacy freely chosen and perpetual for candidates to priestly Ordination in the Latin rite".[176]

Celibacy, in fact, is a gift which the Church has received and desires to retain, convinced that it is a good for the Church itself and for the world.

58. Theological Spiritual Motives of Celibacy

Like any evangelical value, consecrated celibacy should be seen as that liberating novelty which the world, especially today, demands as a radical testimony that following Christ is a sign of the eschatological reality. "Not all can understand it, but only those to whom it has been given. For there are eunuchs who were born so from their mother's womb; and there are eunuchs who were made so by men; and there are eunuchs who have made themselves eunuchs for the kingdom of heaven. He that can understand, let him understand" (*Mt* 19:10-12).[177]

---

[176] JOHN PAUL II Post-Synodal Apostolic Exhortation *Pastores dabo vobis* 29: *l.c.,* 704; cf. ECUMENICAL VATICAN COUNCIL II, Decree *Presbyterorum Ordinis* 16; PAUL VI, Encyclical Letter *Sacerdotalis coelibatus* (24th June 1967), 14: AAS 59 (1967), 662; *C.I.C.*, can. 277, § 1.

[177] Cf. JOHN PAUL 11, Encyclical Letter *Veritatis splendor* (6th August 1993), 22b-c: *AAS* 85 (1993), 1151.

To live with love and generosity the gift received, it is particularly important that the priest understand from the beginning of his seminary formation the theological and spiritual motives of ecclesiastical discipline on celibacy.[178] This particular gift of God demands the observance of chastity, the perfect and perpetual continence for the Kingdom of heaven, so sacred ministers can more easily adhere to Christ with an undivided heart and dedicate themselves more freely to the service of God and man.[179] The ecclesiastical discipline manifests, even before the subject expresses his will to be so disposed, the will of the Church and finds its ultimate reason in the intimate bond which celibacy has with holy Ordination, which shapes the priest to Jesus Christ Head and Spouse of the Church.[180]

The letter to the Ephesians (cf. 5:25-27) shows a strict rapport between the priestly oblation of Christ (cf. 5:25) and the sanctification of the Church (cf. 5:26), loved with a spousal love. Sacramentally inserted into this priesthood of exclusive love of Christ for the Church, his faithful Spouse, the priest expresses this love with his obligation of celibacy, which also becomes a fruitful source of pastoral effectiveness.

Celibacy, therefore, is not an external effect placed upon the priestly ministry, nor can it be simply considered as an institution laid down by law, because those who receive the Sacrament of Holy Orders do so with full freedom and conscience,[181] after years of preparation, and profound reflection and diligent prayer. Along with the firm conviction that Christ grants them this *gift* for the good of the Church and for the service of others, the priest assumes it for his entire life, and it strengthens

---

[178] Cf. ECUMENICAL COUNCIL VATICAN II Decree *Optatam Totius* 10; *C.I.C.*, can. 247 § 1; CONGREGATION FOR CATHOLIC EDUCATION, *Ratio Fundamentalis Institutionis Sacerdotalis* (19th March 1985), 48; *Educational orientation for the formation of priestly celibacy* (11th April 1974), n. 16.

[179] Cf. ECUMENICAL VATICAN COUNCIL II, Decree *Presbyterorum Ordinis* 16; JOHN PAUL II, Letter to Priests for Holy Thursday 1979 *Novo incipiente* (8th April 1979), 8: *AAS* 71 (1979) 405-409; Post-Synodal Apostolic Exhortation *Pastores dabo vobis* 29: *l.c.*, 703-705; *C.I.C.* can. 277 § 1.

[180] Cf. ECUMENICAL COUNCIL VATICAN II, Decree *Presbyterorum Ordinis* 16a; PAUL VI, Encyclical Letter *Sacerdotalis caelibatus* (24th June 1967) 14: *AAS* 59 (1967), 662.

[181] Cf. ECUMENICAL COUNCIL VATICAN II, Decree *Presbyterorum Ordinis* 16c; *C.I.C.* cann. 1036; 1037.

his will with regard to the promise already made during the rite of deaconal Ordination.[182]

For these reasons, ecclesiastical law, on one hand, confirms the gift of celibacy showing it to be in intimate connection with the sacred ministry in its dual dimension of rapport with Christ and with the Church; and, on the other hand, safeguards the freedom of those who assume it.[183] The priest, then, consecrated to Christ with a new exalted title,[184] must be well aware that he has received a gift with a specific juridical bond which he is morally bound to observe. This bond, freely assumed, has theological and moral characteristics which are prior to the juridical characteristics, and is a sign of that spousal reality present in sacramental Ordination. The priest also acquires that true and real spiritual paternity which has universal dimensions, and is specified, in a particular way, in the rapport with the community to which he has been entrusted.[185]

59. Example of Jesus

Celibacy, then, is a gift of self 'in' and 'with' Christ to his Church and expresses the service of the priest to the Church 'in' and 'with' the Lord.[186]

It would be entirely immature to see celibacy as "a tribute to be paid to the Lord" in order to receive Holy Orders rather than 'a gift received through his mercy',[187] as the free and welcomed choice of a particular vocation of love for God and others.

The example is Christ, who in going against what could be considered the dominant culture of his time, freely chose to live celibacy. In following him the disciples left 'everything' to fulfil the mission entrusted to them (*Lk* 18:28-30).

For this reason the Church, from apostolic times, has wished to conserve the gift of perpetual continence of the clergy and choose the

---

[182] Cf. *Pontificale Romanum – De ordinatione Episcopi Presbyterorum et Diaconorum* c. III, 228 (Ed. typica altera 1990), 134; JOHN PAUL II, Letter to Priests for Holy Thursday 1979 *Novo incipiente* (8th April 1979): *AAS* 71 (1979), 409-411.

[183] Cf. SYNOD OF BISHOPS, Document *Ultimis temporibus* (30th November 1971), II, I, 4c: *AAS* 63 (1971), 916-917.

[184] Cf. ECUMENICAL COUNCIL VATICAN II, Decree *Presbyterorum Ordinis* 16b.

[185] Cf. *ibid.*

[186] Cf. JOHN PAUL II, Post-Synodal Apostolic Exhortation *Pastores dabo vobis* 29: *l.c.*, 703-705.

[187] S. CONGREGATION FOR CATHOLIC EDUCATION, *Educative Orientations for the Formation of Ministers to Priestly Celibacy* (11th April 1974), n. 16.

candidates for Holy Orders from among the celibate faithful (cf. 2 *Th* 2:15; 1 *Co* 7:5; 9:5; 1 *Tm* 3:2-12; 5:9; *Ti* 1:6-8).[188]

60. Difficulties and Objections

In today's cultural climate, often conditioned by a vision of man lacking in values and incapable of giving a complete, positive and liberating sense to human sexuality, the question of the value and meaning of priestly celibacy is often presented, or at least the question of its strict rapport with ministerial priesthood.

Difficulties and objections have always accompanied, throughout history, the decision by the Latin Church and some Oriental Churches to confer ministerial priesthood only on those men who have received from God the gift of chastity in celibacy.

The difficulties which some present even today[189] are often founded on pretentious arguments, for example that of an abstracted spiritualism or claiming that continence leads to indifference or disdain for sexuality, or they start from the consideration of difficult and painful cases, or even generalise particular cases. This denies, however, the testimony offered by the great majority of priests, who live their celibacy with internal freedom, rich evangelical motivation, spiritual depth, and in a panorama of strong and joyful fidelity to their vocation and mission.

---

[188] Cf. COUNCIL OF ELVIRA (a. 300-305) cann. 27; 33: BRUNS HERM., *Canones Apostolorum et Conciliorum saec.* IV-VII, II, 5-6; COUNCIL OF NEOCESAREA (a. 314), can. 1; ECUM. COUNCIL OF NICEA I (a 325), can. 3: *Conc. Oecum. Decree* 6; ROMAN SYNOD (a. 386): *Concilia Africae* a. 345-525, *CCl* 149 (in Council of Telepte), 58-63; COUNCIL OF CARTHAGE (a. 390): *ibid* 13. 133 ff.; COUNCIL OF TRULLANO (a. 691), cann. 3, 6, 12, 13, 26, 30, 48: *Pont. Commissio ad redigendum CIC Orientalis* IX I/1 125-186; SIRICIO, decretals *Directa* (a. 386): PL 13, 1131-1147; INNOCENT I, lett. *Dominus inter* (a. 405): BRUNS, cit. 274-277. S. LEO THE GREAT, lett. a Rusticus (a. 456): *PL* 54, 1191; EUSEBIUS OF CESAREA, *Demonstratio Evangelica* 1 9: *PG* 22, 82 (78-83); EPIPHANIO OF SALAMINA, *Panarion PG* 41, 868, 1024; *Expositio Fidei PG* 42, 822-826.

[189] Cf. JOHN PAUL II, Letter to all Priests of the Church on the Occasion of Holy Thursday 1993 (8th April 1993): *AAS* 85 (1993), 880-883; see also *Solo per amore, riflessioni sul celibato sacerdotale*, a cura della Congregasione per il Clero, Ed. Paoline, 1993; *Identità e missione del Sacerdote*, a cura di C. PITTAU – C. SEPE, Ed. Città Nuova 1994.

It is clear that in order to guarantee and protect this gift in a climate of serenity and spiritual progress, possible difficulties for the priests should be avoided by use of appropriate measures.[190]

It is necessary, therefore, that priests conduct themselves with due prudence in dealing with those whose familiarity could be a possible danger for fidelity to this gift or could cause scandal amongst the faithful.[191] In particular cases, he must submit to the judgement of the Bishop, who has the obligation to establish precise rules in this matter.[192]

Priests, then, must not fail to follow those ascetical norms which are proven by the Church's experience and which are demanded even more in present-day circumstances. In this way they may prudently avoid frequenting places, attending shows or reading materials which constitute a danger to the observance of celibate chastity.[193] In making use of means of social communication, whether as pastoral aids or for leisure, they must observe the necessary discretion and avoid anything which could harm their vocation.

To lovingly safeguard the gift received amidst today's climate of irritating sexual permissiveness, they will find in their communion with Christ and with the Church, in their devotion to the Blessed Virgin Mary, and in considering the example of holy priests of all times, the strength necessary to overcome difficulties they may find along their way and act according to that maturity which gives them credence before the world. [194]

---

[190] ST JOHN CHRYSOSTOM, *De Sacerdotio*, VI, 2: *PG* 48, 679: The soul of the priest must be purer than the rays of the sun so that the Holy Spirit not abandon him and so that he might say: *It is no longer I that lives but Christ that lives in me* (*Ga* 2, 20). If the anachorites of the desert who lived far from the city and its activity, enjoying harbour and the tranquility there, they nevertheless did not rely solely on the security of that life of theirs, but rather took special care of strengthening themselves in purity and confidence and diligently insuring to the best of their ability that their conduct be worthy of God's presence. To what extent, do you think, must a priest employ strength and violence to avoid any kind of stain against his spiritual beauty? Certainly he needs to have more purity than monks. Yet precisely he who needs it the most is the one who most often is exposed to inevitable occasions in which he can be contaminated, unless he renders this inaccessible with assiduous sobriety and vigilance.

[191] Cf. *C.I.C.*, can. 277 § 2.

[192] Cf. *ibid.*, can. 277 § 3.

[193] Cf. ECUMENICAL COUNCIL VATICAN II, Decree *Presbyterorum Ordinis* 16c.

[194] Cf. PAUL VI, Encyclical Letter *Sacerdotalis coelibatus* (24th June 1967), 78-81: *AAS* 59 (1967) 688-689; JOHN PAUL II, Post-Synodal Apostolic Exhortation *Pastores dabo vobis*, 29: *l.c.*, 703-705.

Obedience

61. Basis of Obedience

Obedience is a priestly value of primary importance. The very sacrifice of Christ on the Cross acquired salvific value and significance through his obedience and his fidelity to the will of the Father. He was "obedient to death, and death on the Cross" (*Ph* 2:8). The Letter to the Hebrews also points out that Jesus "learned obedience from the things that he suffered" (*Heb* 5:8). It could be said, then, that obedience to the Father is the very heart of the Priesthood of Christ.

Like Christ's, the priest's obedience expresses the will of God which is made manifest to the priest through his legitimate Superiors. This availability must be understood as a true act of personal freedom, the result of a choice continually deepened in the presence of God in prayer. The virtue of obedience, intrinsically required by the sacrament and by the hierarchical structure of the Church, is clearly promised by the clergy, first in the rite of diaconal Ordination, and then in priestly Ordination. With it the priest strengthens his will of submission, thus participating in the dynamics of the obedience of Christ made Servant obedient to death on the Cross (*Ph* 2:7-8).[195]

In contemporary culture the value of the individual's subjectivity and autonomy is emphasised, as if intrinsic to one's dignity. This value, in itself positive, if made absolute and claimed outside of its just context, assumes a negative value.[196] This attitude could also be manifested in ecclesial circles, and in the very life of the priest whenever his activities in the service of the community become reduced to a subjective realm.

In reality, the priest, by the very nature of his ministry, is at the service of Christ and the Church. Therefore, he must be disposed to accept all that is justly indicated by his Superiors and, in a particular way, if not legitimately impeded, must accept and faithfully fulfil the task entrusted to him by his Ordinary.[197]

---

[195] Cf. ECUMENICAL COUNCIL VATICAN II, Decree *Presbyterorum Ordinis*, 15c; JOHN PAUL II, Post-Synodal Apostolic Exhortation *Pastores dabo vobis*, 27: *l.c.*, 700-701.

[196] Cf. JOHN PAUL II, Encyclical Letter *Veritatis splendor* (6th August 1993), 31; 32; 106: *AAS* 85 (1993), 1159-1160; 1216.

[197] Cf. *C.I.C.*, can. 274 § 2.

62. *Hierarchical Obedience*

Priests have a "special obligation to show reverence and obedience to the Supreme Pontiff and to their own Ordinary."[198] In virtue of his belonging to a determined presbyterate, the priest is charged with the service of a particular Church, in which the principle and foundation of unity is the Bishop[199] who has all the ordinary, proper and immediate authority required for the exercise of his pastoral office.[200] This hierarchical subordination, required by the sacrament of Holy Orders, finds its ecclesiological-structural fulfilment in reference to one's own Bishop and to the Roman Pontiff, ordinary of the universal Church and thus of each particular Church.[201]

The obligation to follow the Magisterium in matters of faith and morals is intrinsically united to all the functions which the priest must perform in the Church. Dissent in this area is to be considered grave, in that it produces scandal and confusion among the faithful.

No one is more aware than the priest of the fact that the Church needs norms. In fact, since the Church's hierarchical and organic structure is visible, the exercise of its functions, divinely entrusted, especially those concerning its guidance and the celebration of the sacraments, must be adequately organised.[202]

As for the ministry of Christ and of his Church, the priest generously takes on the duty to faithfully fulfil each and every norm, avoiding any sense of partial compliance according to subjective criteria, which creates division and has damaging effects upon the lay faithful and public opinion. Indeed, "canonical laws, by their very nature, demand observance" and require "that which is mandated by the head be observed by the members".[203]

---

[198] Cf. *C.I.C.*, can. 273.

[199] Cf. ECUMENICAL VATICAN COUNCIL II, DOGMATIC CONSTITUTION *Lumen gentium*, 23a.

[200] Cf. *ibid*, 27a; *C.I.C.*, can. 381 § 1.

[201] Cf. ECUMENICAL COUNCIL VATICAN II, Decr. *Christus Dominus*, 2a; Dogm. Const. *Lumen gentium*, 22b; *C.I.C.*, can. 333 § 1.

[202] Cf. JOHN PAUL II, Apostolic Const. *Sacrae disciplinae leges* (25th January 1983): *AAS* 75 (1983) Pars II, XIII; *Address* to the participants of the International Symposium *"Ius in vita et in missione Ecclesiae"* (23rd April 1993), in "L'Osservatore Romano", 25th April 1993.

[203] Cf. JOHN PAUL II, Apostolic Const. *Sacrae disciplinae leges* (25th January 1983): *AAS* 75 (1983) Pars II, XIII

In obeying the constituted authority, the priest, furthermore, enhances mutual charity within the priesthood and also enhances that unity which has its foundation in the truth.

63. Authority Exercised with Charity

In order to achieve a real obedience which will nourish ecclesial communion, those who are in authority (Ordinaries, religious Superiors, Moderators of societies of apostolic life), other than offer their necessary and constant personal example, must exercise their own institutional office with charity, be it in anticipating or properly requesting the adhesion to each disposition *in the magisterial and disciplinarian realm*.[204]

Such obedience is a source of freedom, insofar as it stimulates sincere growth in maturity in the priest, who will know how to assume a serene and even-minded pastoral conduct, creating a harmony in which personality is based on a deep unity.

64. Respect for the Liturgical Norms

Among the many aspects of the question, the one concerning liturgical norms merits special attention in our times.

Liturgy is the exercise of the priesthood of Jesus Christ,[205] "the summit to which all action of the Church is directed; it is also the fount from which all her power flows".[206] This constitutes an ambit in which the priest should have particular awareness of being a minister and faithfully obeying the Church. "The ordering and guidance of the sacred liturgy depends solely on the authority of the Church, namely, that of the Apostolic See, and, as provided by law, that of the diocesan Bishop".[207] Therefore, in such matter, he must not add, remove or change anything by his own initiative.[208]

This is especially true for the celebration of the sacraments, which are acts of Christ and the Church by excellence, and which the priest administers in the person of Christ and in name of the Church for the good

---

[204] Cf. *C.I.C.* can. 3w.

[205] Cf. ECUMENICAL COUNCIL VATICAN II, Cost. *Sacrosanctum Concilium*, 7.

[206] *Ibid.* 10.

[207] *C.I.C.*, can. 838.

[208] Cf. ECUMENICAL VATICAN COUNCIL II, Constitution *Sacrosanctum Concilium*, 22.

of the faithful.[209] These have a true right to participate in the liturgical celebrations as the Church wills and not according to the personal likes of a particular minister, nor according to unapproved and unusual rites, expressions of specific groups which tend to cut themselves off from the universality of the People of God.

65. *Unity in Pastoral Planning*

It is essential that priests, in exercising their ministry, not only participate responsibly in the creation of pastoral plans which the Bishop (with the co-operation with the Council of Priests)[210] determines; they must also develop their own communities in harmony with these plans.

Creativity, that spirit of initiative proper to a well formed priest, will not only be unrestrained but can also be used to full advantage in pastoral effectiveness.

An erroneous sense of independence in this area could bring about not only a rupture in the necessary communion, but a weakening of the very work of evangelisation as well.

66. *Obligation of Ecclesiastical Attire*

In a secularised and materialistic society, where the external signs of sacred and supernatural realities tend to disappear, it is particularly important that the community be able to recognise the priest, man of God and dispenser of his mysteries, by his attire as well, which is an unequivocal sign of his dedication and his identity as a public minister.[211] The priest should be identifiable primarily through his conduct, but also by his manner of dressing, which makes visible to all the faithful, indeed and to all men,[212] his identity and his belonging to God and the Church.

For this reason, the clergy should wear "suitable ecclesiastical dress, in accordance with the norms established by the Episcopal Conference

---

[209] Cf. *C.I.C.*, can. 846 § 1.

[210] Cf. SACRED CONGREGATION FOR THE CLERGY, Circular letter *Omnis Christifideles* (25th January 1973), 9.

[211] Cf. JOHN PAUL II, Letter to the Cardinal Vicar of Rome (8th September 1982): "L'Osservatore Romano", 18th-19th October 1982.

[212] Cf. PAUL VI, Allocution to Clergy (17th February 1969; 17th February 1972; 10th February 1978): *AAS* 61 (1969), 190; 64 (1972), 223; 70 (1978), 191; JOHN PAUL II, Letter to All Priests on the Occasion of Holy Thursday 1979 *Novo incipiente* (7th April 1979), 7: *AAS* 71 403-405; Allocutions to Clergy (9th November 1978; 19th April 1979); *Insegnamenti*, I (1978), 116; II (1979), 929.

and the legitimate local custom".[213] This means that the attire, when it is not the cassock, must be different from the manner in which the laity dress, and conform to the dignity and sacredness of his ministry. The style and colour should be established by the Episcopal Conference, always in agreement with the dispositions of the universal law.

Because of their incoherence with the spirit of this discipline, contrary practices cannot be considered legitimate customs; and should be removed by the competent authority.[214]

Outside of entirely exceptional cases, a cleric's failure to use this proper ecclesiastical attire could manifest a weak sense of his identity as one consecrated to God.[215]

Priestly Spirit of Poverty

67. Poverty as Availability

The poverty of Christ has a salvific scope. Christ, being rich, became poor for us, that by his poverty we might become rich (cf. 2 *Co* 8:9).

The letter to the Philippians reveals the rapport between the giving of oneself and the spirit of service which should enliven the pastoral ministry. St Paul says that Jesus did not consider "being equal to God a thing to be clung to, but emptied himself, taking the nature of a slave" (*Ph* 2:6-7). A priest could hardly be a true servant and minister of his brothers if he were excessively worried with his comfort and well-being.

Through his condition of poverty, Christ manifested that he has received everything from eternity from the Father and all to him is restored in a complete offering of his life.

The example of Christ should lead the priest to conform himself to him, with an interior detachment as to the goods and riches of the world.[216] The

---

[213] *C.I.C.*, can. 284.

[214] Cf. PAUL VI, Motu Proprio *Ecclesiae Sanctae*, I, 25, § 2d: AAS 58 (1966), 770; SACRED CONGREGATION OF BISHOPS, Circular Letter to all pontifical representatives *Per venire incontro* (27th January 1976); SACRED CONGREGATION FOR CATHOLIC EDUCATION, Circular Letter *The document* (6th January 1980): "L'Osservatore Romano" suppl., 12th April 1980.

[215] Cf. PAUL VI, *Catechism* in the General Audience of 17th September 1969; Allocution to Clergy (1st March 1973): *Insegnamenti*, VII (1969), 1065; XI (1973), 176.

[216] Cf. ECUMENICAL COUNCIL VATICAN II, Decr. *Presbyterorum Ordinis*, 17 a.d; 20-21.

Lord teaches us that the true goodness is God and that true richness is reaching eternal life: "For what does it profit a man, if he gain the whole world, but suffer the loss of his own soul? Or what will a man give in exchange for his soul?" (*Mk* 8:36-37).

The priest, whose inheritance is the Lord (*Nb* 18:20), knows that his mission, like that of the Church, is carried out in the middle of the world and that created goods are necessary for the personal development of man. However, he will use these goods with a sense of responsibility, moderation, upright intention and detachment, precisely because he has his treasure in heaven and knows that all should be used for building the Kingdom of God (*Lk* 10:7; *Mt* 10:9-10; 1 *Co* 9:14; *Ga* 6:6).[217] Therefore, the priest will deny himself those worldly activities which are not in keeping with his ministry.[218]

Remembering, moreover, that the gift he has received is gratuitous, he must be disposed to give in like manner (*Mt* 10:8; *Ac* 8:18-25),[219] and to use what he receives from the exercise of his office for the good of the Church and works of charity, after having provided for his honest sustenance.[220]

The priest, although not having assumed poverty as a public promise, must lead a simple life and avoid anything which could have an air of vanity,[221] voluntarily embracing poverty to follow Christ more closely.[222] In all aspects (living quarters, means of transportation, vacations, etc.), the priest must eliminate any kind of affectation and luxury.[223]

Friend of those most in need, he will reserve his most refined pastoral charity for these, with a preferential option for all poverty, old and new, tragically present in our world, always remembering that the first misery from which man must be liberated is that of sin, the root of all evil.

---

[217] Cf. *ibid.*, 17 a.c; JOHN PAUL II, *Caterchesi* in the General Audience of 21st July 1993, n. 3: "L'Osservatore Romano", 22nd July 1993.

[218] Cf. *C.I.C.*, can. 286; 1392.

[219] Cf. ECUMENICAL COUNCIL VATICAN II, Decree *Presbyterorum Ordinis*, 17d.

[220] Cf. *ibid.*, 17c; *C.I.C.*, cann. 282; 222, § 2; 529, § 1

[221] Cf. *C.I.C.*, can. 282, § 1.

[222] Cf. ECUMENICAL COUNCIL VATICAN 11, Decree *Presbyterorum Ordinis*,17d.

[223] Cf. *ibid.*, 17e.

Devotion to Mary

68. Imitating the Virtues of our Mother

There is an "essential rapport... between the Mother of Jesus and the priesthood of the ministry of the Son", stemming from the existing one between the divine maternity of Mary and the priesthood of Christ.[224]

In light of such a rapport, Marian spirituality is rooted in every priest. Priestly spirituality could not be considered complete if it were to fail to include the message of Christ's words on the Cross, in which he conferred his Mother to the beloved disciple, and, through him, to all priests called to continue his work of redemption.

Like John at the foot of the Cross, every priest has been entrusted, in a special way, with Mary as Mother (cf. *Jn* 19:26-27).

Priests, who are among the favoured disciples of Jesus, crucified and risen, should welcome Mary as their Mother in their own life, bestowing her with constant attention and prayer. The Blessed Virgin then becomes the Mother who leads them to Christ, who makes them sincerely love the Church, who intercedes for them and who guides them toward the Kingdom of heaven.

Every priest knows that Mary, as Mother, is also the most distinguished modeller of his priesthood, since it is she who moulds the priestly soul, protects it from dangers, from routine and discouragement, and maternally safeguards it, so he may grow in wisdom, age and grace, before God and men (cf. *Lk* 2:40).

But they are not devout sons if they do not know how to imitate the virtues of Mary. The priest will look to Mary to be a humble, obedient and chaste minister and to give testimony of charity in the total surrender to God and to the Church.[225]

Masterpiece of the priestly Sacrifice of Christ, the Blessed Virgin represents the Church in the purest way, "with neither stain nor blemish", completely "holy and immaculate" (*Ep* 5:27). This contemplation of the Blessed Virgin places before the priest the ideal to which the ministry in his community should lead, so that this be a "wholly glorious Church" (*ibid.*) through the priestly gift of his very life.

---

[224] Cf. JOHN PAUL II, *Catechesi* in the General Audience of 30th June 1993: "L'Osservatore Romano, 30th June-1st July 1993".

[225] ECUMENICAL COUNCIL VATICAN II, Decree *Presbytrorum Ordinis*, 18b.

CHAPTER III

ONGOING FORMATION

Principles

69. The Need for Ongoing formation Today

Ongoing formation is a need which begins and develops from the moment of receiving the Sacrament of Holy Orders: with it the priest is not only 'consecrated' by the Father and 'sent' by the Son, but also 'animated' by the Holy Spirit. Hence, permanent formation springs from a Grace which produces a supernatural force destined to assimilate continually, in ever broader and deeper terms, the entire life and activity of the priest in fidelity to the gift received: "I am reminding you," writes St Paul to Timothy, "to fan into a flame the gift that God gave you" (2 *Tm* 1:6).

This necessity is intrinsic to the divine gift itself,[226] which is continually 'vivified' so that the priest may adequately respond to his vocation. As a man situated in history, he needs to perfect himself in all the aspects of his human and spiritual existence in order to attain that conformity with Christ, the unifying principle of all things.

Rapid and widespread transformations and a secularised social fabric typical of the contemporary world are what make unavoidable the priest's duty of being adequately prepared, so that he not lose his own identity and so that he might respond to the demands of the new evangelisation. To this grave duty corresponds the specific right of the faithful, who feel the effects of priests' solid formation and sanctity in a definite way.[227]

70. A Continuous Task

The spiritual life of the priest and his pastoral ministry go hand in hand with that ongoing personal formation to deepen and harmonise the human, spiritual, intellectual, and pastoral aspects of his formation. This task, which should begin in the seminary, must be supported by the Bishops at various levels: national, regional and, above all, diocesan.

---

[226] Cf. JOHN PAUL II, Post-Synodal Apostolic Exhortation *Pastores dabo vobis*, 70: *l.c.*, 778-782.

[227] Cf. *ibid.*

It is encouraging to note that there are already many Dioceses and Episcopal Conferences involved in promising initiatives aimed at enhancing an authentic permanent formation of their own priests. It is hoped that all Dioceses may be able to respond to this need. However, where this may be impossible for the moment, it is advisable that they come to an agreement among themselves or contact those institutions or persons especially prepared to handle such a delicate task.[228]

71. Instruments of Sanctification

Ongoing formation presents itself as a necessary means to the priest of today in order to achieve the aim of his vocation: the service of God and of his People.

In practice, this consists in helping all priests respond generously to the commitment demanded by the dignity and the responsibility which God conferred upon them through the sacrament of Orders; in guarding, defending, and developing their specific identity and vocation; and in sanctifying themselves and others through the exercise of their ministry.

This means that priests must avoid any dualism between spirituality and ministry, for it is at the origin of some profound crises.

It is evident that in order to achieve this end of a supernatural order, the general criteria on which the permanent formation of priests is to be organised must be discovered and analysed.

Such general principles must be developed in light of the end proposed for the process of formation.

72. It Must be Imparted by the Church

Ongoing formation is a right-duty of the priest and imparting it is a right-duty of the Church. This is established in universal law.[229] In fact, in the same way that the vocation to the sacred ministry is received in the Church, only the Church has the competence to impart the specific formation according to the responsibility proper to such ministry. Therefore, permanent formation – an activity linked to the exercise of the ministerial priesthood – belongs to the responsibility of the Pope and of the Bishops. The Church, then, has the duty and the right to continue forming its ministers, helping them to progress in generous response to the gift which God has bestowed upon them.

---

[228] Cf. *ibid*, 79: *l.c.*, 797.

[229] Cf. *C.I.C.*, can. 279.

On his part, the minister has also received, as a demand of the gift connected with Ordination, the right to have the necessary help from the Church in order to carry out his service effectively and in a holy way.

73. It Must be Ongoing

The activity of formation is based on a dynamic demand intrinsic to the ministerial charisma, which is permanent and irreversible in itself. Therefore this can never be considered finished, neither on the part of the Church which imparts it, nor on the part of the minister who receives it. It is therefore necessary that this be thought of and developed in such a way that all priests may receive it *always*, keeping in mind the characteristics and possibilities that vary with age, condition of life, and assignments.[230]

74. It Must be Complete

Such a formation must cover and harmonise all the dimensions of the formation of priests. Thus, it must tend to help each priest achieve the development of a full human personality matured in the spirit of service to others, in whatever task he may receive; it will permit him to be intellectually prepared in the theological sciences as well as in the human sciences, insofar as they are linked with his ministry, in order to pursue his function as witness to the faith with a greater effectiveness; that he have a deep spiritual life, nourished by intimacy with Jesus Christ and by love for the Church; and so that he may pursue his pastoral ministry with zeal and dedication.

In practice, such formation must be complete: spiritual, pastoral, human, intellectual, systematic and personalised.

75. Human Formation

This formation is extremely important in today's world, as it always has been. The priest must never forget that he is a man chosen among men to be at the service of men.

To sanctify himself and carry out his priestly mission, he must present himself with an abundance of human virtues which render him worthy of esteem by those around him.

---

[230] Cf. JOHN PAUL II, Post-Synodal Apostolic Exhortation *Pastores dabo vobis*, 76: *l.c.*, 793-794.

In particular he must practice goodness of heart, patience, kindness, strength of soul, love for justice, even-mindedness, truthfulness to his word, coherence in the duties freely assumed, etc.[231]

It is likewise important that human virtues be reflected in the priest's social conduct, correctness in the various forms of human relations, friendships, courtesy, etc.

76. Spiritual Formation

Keeping in mind all that has been said with regards to spiritual life, we limit ourselves here to presenting some practical means of formation.

Above all, it would be necessary to deepen the understanding of the principal aspects of priestly existence, especially referring to the biblical, patristic and hagiographic teachings in which the priest must continually update himself, not only by reading good books but also by participating in courses of studies, congresses, etc.[232]

Specific sessions may be dedicated to the care exercised in the celebration of the Sacraments as well as to the study of questions of spirituality such as Christian and human virtues, ways of praying, rapport between spiritual life and liturgical ministry, pastoral ministry, etc.

More particularly, it is hoped that each priest, perhaps during spiritual retreats, would develop a concrete plan of life, possibly in agreement with his own spiritual director. The following points may be indicated: 1. daily meditation on the Word or on a mystery of the Faith; 2. daily personal encounter with Jesus Christ in the Eucharist apart from the devout celebration of the Holy Mass; 3. Marian devotion (Rosary, consecration or offering, intimate conversation); 4. periods of doctrinal formation and study of hagiography; 5. due rest; 6. renewed effort to put into practice the indications of the Bishop and to verify his convictions of adherence to the Magisterium and to ecclesiastical discipline and; 7. care for his communion and friendship with other priests.

77. Intellectual Formation

Considering the enormous influence which humanistic and philosophical trends have on modern culture, as well as the fact that some priests have not

---

[231] Cf. ECUMENICAL VATICAN COUNCIL II, Decree *Presbyterorum Ordinis*, 3.

[232] Cf. ECUMENICAL COUNCIL VATICAN II, Decree *Presbyterorum Ordinis*, 19; Decree *Optatam Totitus*, 22, *C.I.C.* can. 279, § 2, CONGREGATION FOR CATHOLIC EDUCATION *Ratio Fundamentalis Institutionis Sacerdotalis* (19th March 1985), 101.

received an adequate preparation in such disciplines, and also because they come from different scholarly backgrounds, it is necessary that these meetings deal with the more relevant humanistic and philosophical themes or those that are "linked to the sacred sciences, particularly insofar as they benefit the exercise of the pastoral ministry".[233] Such themes also constitute a valid aid in order to deal correctly with the principal arguments of fundamental, dogmatic and moral theology, of Sacred Scriptures, of Liturgy, of Canon Law and of Ecumenism, etc., bearing in mind that the teaching of these matters should not be simply problematic, informative and theoretical but must lead to an authentic formation: towards prayer, communion and pastoral action.

Things should be done in such a way that during priestly encounters the documents of the Magisterium may be studied together in a profound manner, under an authoritative guide, so that the unity of interpretation and practice – so useful in the work of evangelisation – may be facilitated in the pastoral work of the Dioceses.

Particular importance in intellectual formation must be given to the handling of themes which today have more relevance in cultural debates and pastoral practices, such as, for example, those related to social ethics, bioethics, etc.

A special treatment must be reserved to the questions posed by scientific advances, which are especially influential to the mentality of contemporary men. Priests must be up-to-date and prepared to respond to questions that science may pose in its advancement. They should not fail to consult well-grounded and sound experts.

It is of the greatest interest that the social doctrine of the Church be studied, deepened and disseminated. The interests of the priests who are in favour of the needy, and of all the faithful through them, must not remain as mere desires but be converted into specific efforts, always following the impulse of the magisterial teachings. "Today more than ever the Church is aware that her social message must find credibility in the *testimony of works*, first of all in her internal coherence and logic".[234]

An indispensable demand for the intellectual formation of priests is the knowledge and use of the *means of social communications*. These means, if well used, constitute a providential instrument of evangelisation,

---

[233] *C.I.C.*, Can. 279, § 3.

[234] Cf. JOHN PAUL II, Encycl.. Letter *Centesimus annus* (1st May 1991), 57: *AAS* 83 (1991), 862-863

capable of reaching not only great masses of faithful but also of leaving a mark on their minds and behaviour.

In this regard it would be opportune that the Bishop or the Episcopal Conference itself prepare programs and technical instruments appropriate for this goal.

78. Pastoral Formation

For an adequate pastoral formation, it is necessary to organise encounters in which the principle objective is the reflection upon the pastoral plan of the Diocese. In these, the consideration of all questions pertinent to the priest's pastoral life and practice (fundamental morals, and professional and social ethics, among others) should not be disregarded.

Special care must be devoted to understanding the life and spirituality of the permanent deacons – where they exist, as well as of the religious and of the lay faithful.

Other themes which could be helpful are those dealing with catechesis, the family, vocations to priesthood and religious life, youth, the elderly, the sick, ecumenism and the 'the fallen away'.

For pastoral work in present circumstances, it is very important that special sessions be devoted to exploring and assimilating the *Catechism of the Catholic Church*. Especially for priests, this constitutes a precious instrument of formation for preaching as well as for works of evangelisation in general.

79. It must be Systematic

For pastoral formation to be complete, it must be organised "not as something haphazard, but as a systematic offering of subjects, which unfolds by stages and take on precise forms".[235] This requires a certain organising structure which will establish opportune instruments, times and contents for its particular and adequate realisation.

Such organisation must be accompanied by the habit of personal study, since periodic courses would be of little use if not accompanied by serious study.[236]

80. It must be Personalised

Although it may be for all, ongoing formation has, as its direct objective, service to those who receive it. Thus, together with the collective or

---

[235] JOHN PAUL II, Post-Synodal Apostolic Exhortation *Pastores dabo vobis* 79: *l.c.* 797.
[236] Cf. *ibid.*

common means of formation, there must also be other means which truly personalise the formation of each one.

For this reason, there should be an awareness, especially on the part of those responsible, that all priests must be reached personally, taking care of each one, and not simply having all the diverse opportunities available to them.

In his turn, each priest must feel encouraged to assume responsibility for his own formation, with the word and example of his Bishop and of his brothers in the priesthood, himself being the first agent of his own formation.[237]

Organisation

81. Priestly Encounters

The itinerary of priestly encounters must have a unitary character and progress by stages.

Such unity must converge in the conformation with Christ in a way that the truth of faith, spiritual life and ministerial activity may work towards a gradual maturity of the entire priesthood.

The unified formative path is divided into well-defined stages. This requires a specific attention to the different phases of the life of the priest, without ignoring any stage, and taking care to unite common formative means with those that are personal.

The encounters of priests should be considered necessary in order to grow in communion, for a growing consciousness and adequate scrutiny of the problems corresponding to each stage of life.

Regarding the content of such meetings, we can refer here to the themes proposed by the national or regional Episcopal Conferences. In every case, themes must be established in a precise plan of formation by the Diocese, and frequently updated, possibly even every year.[238]

Their organisation and development may be prudently entrusted by the Bishop to the faculty or institute of theological and pastoral studies, to the seminary, to organisations or federations involved in the formation of priests,[239] or to other specialised centres or institutes which may be diocesan, regional or national, provided that their doctrinal orthodoxy,

---

[237] Cf. ibid.

[238] Cf. ibid.

[239] Cf. ibid.; ECUMENICAL COUNCIL VATICAN II, Decree Optatam Totius 22; Decree Presbyterorum Ordinis 19c.

fidelity to the Magisterium and ecclesiastical discipline are assured, as well as their scientific competence and their adequate knowledge of real pastoral situations.

82. Pastoral Year

It will be the task of the Bishop to see to it, through prudently-chosen help, that in the year following the priestly or deaconal Ordination a so-called pastoral year be established, which will ease the passage from the seminary life to the exercise of the sacred ministry, proceeding gradually and facilitating a progressive and harmonious human and specifically priestly maturation.[240]

In the course of this year, it will be necessary to ensure that the newly ordained priests not be immersed in excessively burdensome and delicate situations such as far off destinations away from their brothers. Instead, it would be good that some opportune form of common life be facilitated.

This period of formation may be held in a suitable residence established for this purpose (House of Clerics) or in a place which may constitute a precise and serene point for all priests during their early pastoral experiences. This will facilitate conversation and meeting with the Bishop and with one's brothers, common prayers (Liturgy of the Hours, Eucharistic adoration, Holy Rosary, etc.), exchange of experiences, mutual encouragement, and the start of good relations of friendship.

It would be convenient for the Bishop to introduce new priests in the beginning of their ministry to priests of exemplary life and pastoral zeal. Notwithstanding the often critical pastoral needs, the first assignment must respond, above all, to the need of setting the young priests on the right road. The sacrifice of a year may then bear fruit for a long time in the future.

It is not superfluous to underline the fact that this year, both delicate and valuable must favour the full growth of a rapport between the priest and his Bishop which, initiated in the seminary, ought to become a true father and son relationship.

In what refers to the intellectual aspect, this year must not be filled with learning new material but rather involve a deep assimilation of all that

---

[240] Cf. PAUL VI, Motu Proprio *Ecclesiae Sanctae* (6th August 1966), I, 7: *AAS* 58 (1966), 761; S. CONGREGATION FOR THE CLERGY, Circular Letter to the Presidents of the Episcopal Conferences *Inter ea* (4th November 1969), 16: *AAS* 62 (1970), 130-131; CONGREGATION FOR CATHOLIC EDUCATION, *Ratio Fundamentalis Institutiones Sacerdotalis* (19th March 1985), 63; 101; *C.I.C.* can. 1032, § 2.

was studied in the institutional courses so as to favour the formation of a mentality capable of appreciating the details in the light of God's design.[241]

In this context, there may be properly organised lessons and seminars on the practice of confession, liturgy, catechetics and preaching, canon law, spirituality of priests, lay people and religious, social doctrine, communication and its means, a knowledge of sects and new religious trends.

In practice, the work of synthesis must constitute the path on which the pastoral year is directed. Every element must correspond to the fundamental aim of maturing in the spiritual life.

The success of the pastoral year is in any case always conditioned by the daily personal effort of the one concerned to seek sanctity and to use the means of sanctification which have helped him since his seminary days.

Means

83. 'Sabbatical' Periods

Among other factors that may cause discouragement in the souls of pastors are the danger of routine, physical exhaustion due to overwork, psychological fatigue caused by having to struggle against misunderstanding, prejudice, going against organised forces that tend to give the impression that the priests of today belong to a culturally obsolete minority.

Notwithstanding pastoral urgency, and precisely to face up to these problems adequately, priests must be provided with time, as much as reasonably possible, so as to facilitate longer periods spent with the Lord Jesus, thus recovering strength and courage to continue the road to holiness.

To respond to this particular demand, in many Dioceses various initiatives have already been tested – often with promising results.

These results are valid and may be taken into consideration, despite the difficulties that may be encountered in some areas where the scarcity of priests is more acutely felt.

For this purpose, monasteries, sanctuaries or other places of spirituality, which are far from the main urban centres, may lend a helping hand in sparing the priest from direct pastoral responsibilities.

In some cases, it may be useful to employ this time for study or updating oneself in the sacred sciences, yet the primary goal of strengthening spiritual and apostolic life must not be forgotten.

---

[241] Cf. CONGREGATION FOR CATHOLIC EDUCATION, *Ratio Fundamentalis Institutiones Sacerdotalis* (19th March 1985), 63.

In any case, the danger of considering the sabbatical period as vacation time or claiming it as a right should be avoided.

84. House for Clerics

A 'House for Clerics' is to be desired when possible, for holding the above-mentioned formative encounters and also as a reference place for other various circumstances. Such a house should offer all the organisational structure which will make it comfortable and attractive.

Where they do not yet exist but necessity suggests it, it is advisable to create either on a national or regional level, structures suitable for the physical, psychological, and spiritual recovery of priests in special need.

85. Retreats and Recollections

As the long spiritual experience of the Church shows, retreats and recollections are suitable and effective instruments for an adequate permanent formation of priests. These still maintain their necessity and relevance. Against a practice that tends to empty man of everything that is interior, the priest must find God inside himself, taking advantage of spiritual pauses in order to immerse himself in meditation and in prayer.

For this reason, canonical legislation has established that clerics: "are obliged to make spiritual retreats, in accordance with the provisions of particular law".[242] The two most usual modes which may be prescribed by the Bishop in his own Diocese are the day of recollection (possibly monthly) and the annual Retreat.

It is fitting that the Bishop plan and organise the retreats and recollections in such a way that each priest has the possibility of choosing those retreats, usually done within or outside of his Diocese, given by exemplary priests or by a religious institution especially experienced for their charisma in spiritual formation, or within monasteries.

Organising a special retreat for priests ordained in recent years is also advisable, in which the Bishop himself may actively participate.[243]

During such encounters, it is important to focus on spiritual themes, offer long periods of silence and prayer, and to take special care in the celebration of the liturgy, the Sacrament of Penance, Eucharistic

---

[242] *C.I.C.*, can 276, § 2, 4; cf. can. 533, § 2; 550, § 3.

[243] Cf. S. CONGREGATION FOR CATHOLIC EDUCATION, Ratio *Fundamentalis Institutiones Sacerdotalis* (19th March 1985), 101.

adoration, spiritual direction and acts of veneration and cult to the Blessed Virgin Mary.

To give greater importance to the efficacy of these means of formation, the Bishop may duly name a priest to take charge of organising the times and the way of conducting them.

In each case, it is necessary that days of recollection and especially annual spiritual retreats be seen as times of prayer and not as courses of theological-pastoral updating.

86. The Need for Programming

Recognising the difficulties that permanent formation usually encounters, above all due to the multiple and burdensome tasks that priests have, it must be said that all these difficulties are surmountable if they are carried out responsibly.

To be in keeping with the level of circumstances and confront the demands of the urgent work of evangelisation, a courageous action of pastoral government must be undertaken which is designed to take care of priests in a very particular way. It is necessary that the Bishops demand, with the force of charity, that their priests be generous in following the legitimate dispositions made in this matter.

The existence of a "plan of permanent formation" requires that this be not only thought of or planned but also carried out. In this regard a clear work structure is called for: with *objectives, specific topics and instruments* to carry them out.

Those Responsible

87. The Priest

It is the priest himself who is the person primarily responsible for ongoing formation. In reality, this duty of being faithful to the gift of God and to the dynamism of daily conversion falls upon each priest.[244]

Such a duty is derived from the fact that no one can take the place of the priest in watching over himself (cf. 1 *Tm* 4:16). In fact, by participating in the unique priesthood of Christ, he is called by his irrepeatable vocation to reveal and exercise the extraordinary richness of grace which he has received.

---

[244] Cf. JOHN PAUL II, Post-Synodal Apostolic Exhortation *Pastores dabo vobis*, 70: *l.c.,* 778-782.

On the other hand, the conditions and situations of life of every single priest are such that, even from the merely human point of view, he must involve himself in his own formation, in a manner which takes advantage of his own capacities and possibilities.

He, therefore, should participate actively in the formative encounters, making his own contribution based on his capacities and specific talents and will strive to furnish himself with books and magazines with sound doctrine and of proven utility, for his spiritual life and the fruitful development of his ministry.

Among his reading material, the primary place must be given to Sacred Scripture; and then the writings of the Fathers, classical and modern spiritual Masters, and the Documents of the Magisterium, which constitute the authoritative and updated source of permanent formation. Priests should study them and deepen their understanding of them (directly and personally) in order to adequately present them to the lay faithful.

88. *Brotherly Assistance*

In all the aspects of priestly existence there appear particular bonds of apostolic charity, of ministry and of fraternity,[245] which serve as the foundation of the reciprocal help that priests give each other.[246] It is to be hoped that co-operation among all priests should grow and develop as regards their spiritual and human life, as well as their ministerial service. The help which must be given to priests in this field can find support in the different priestly associations which tend to form a truly diocesan spirituality. This regards those associations whose "statutes are recognised by the competent authority and which, by a suitable and well tried rule of life and by fraternal support, promote holiness in the exercise of their ministry and foster the unity of the clergy with one another and with their Bishop".[247]

In this perspective, the right of every diocesan priest to plan his own spiritual life must be respected with great care, obviously in keeping with the characteristics of his own vocation and the obligations that derive from it.

---

[245] ECUMENICAL COUNCIL VATICAN II, Decree *Presbyterorum Ordinis*, 8.

[246] Cf. *ibid.*

[247] *C.I.C.*, can. 278, § 2; cf. ECUMENICAL VATICAN COUNCIL II, Decree *Presbyterorum Ordinis*, 8.

The work that these associations and other approved movements carry out for priests, is held in high esteem by the Church,[248] who recognises this as a sign of the of vitality with which the Holy Spirit continually renews her.

89. The Bishop

However ample and arduous the work with that portion of the People of God entrusted to him may be, the Bishop must observe a very special diligence in all that refers to the permanent formation of his priests.[249]

In fact, a special relationship exists between them and the Bishop, due to "the fact that priests receive their priesthood from him and share his pastoral solicitude for the People of God".[250] Thus it also constitutes a specific responsibility of the Bishop in the area of priestly formation.

Such responsibility is expressed both in that which concerns the individual priest, for whom the formation must be as personalised as possible, and in that which concerns the formation of all the priests who make up the diocesan presbyterium. In this sense, the Bishop will never fail to foster communication and communion among priests, taking particular care, to guard and promote the true nature of their ongoing formation, to educate their consciences regarding its necessity and importance, and finally, to plan the necessary structure and appropriate persons to carry it out.[251]

In providing for the formation of his priests, the Bishop must be involved in his own personal and permanent formation. Experience teaches that the more the Bishop is bent on his own formation and convinced of its primary importance, the more he will know how to encourage and sustain that of his clergy.

In this delicate work the Bishop, while performing an irreplaceable and undelegatable role, will know how to seek the collaboration of the council of priests, for it is an organism which, by its nature and purpose, is a suitable aid, especially in certain tasks such as that of drawing up the plan of formation.

---

[248] Cf. ECUMENICAL COUNCIL VATICAN II, Decree *Presbyterorum Ordinis*, 8; *C.I.C.*, can. 278, § 2; JOHN PAUL II, Post-Synodal Apostolic Exhortation Pastores *dabo vobis*, 81: *l.c.*, 799-800.

[249] Cf. ECUMENICAL COUNCIL VATICAN II, Decree *Christum Dominus*, 16d.

[250] JOHN PAUL II, Post-Synodal Apostolic Exhortation *Pastores dabo vobis*, 79: *l.c.*, 797.

[251] Cf. *ibid.*: *l.c.*, 797-798.

Every Bishop, then, will feel himself supported and helped in his task by his brothers in the Episcopate, united in the Conference.[252]

90. Formation of Directors

No formation is possible without both the person who must be formed and the subject who forms: the director. The quality and the effectiveness of a plan of formation will depend partially on the organisation, and principally on the directors.

It is obvious that the responsibility of the Bishop is even more significant with regards to their formation.

It is necessary, therefore, that the Bishop himself name a 'group of directors' and that these persons be selected among those priests who are highly qualified and esteemed due to their background and their human, spiritual, cultural and pastoral maturity.

In fact, the directors must be, above all, men of prayer: teachers with a strong supernatural outlook, a profound spiritual life, of exemplary conduct, with adequate experience in the priestly ministry, capable of consolidating the priest's spiritual demands with those properly human and like the Fathers of the Church and great saints of all times. They may also be Chosen from among the members of the seminary, centres or academic institutions approved by the ecclesiastical authority, including those institutions whose charisma concerns the life and spirituality of priests. In any case, doctrinal orthodoxy and faithfulness to the ecclesiastical disciplines must be guaranteed. Moreover, the directors must be trustworthy collaborators of the Bishop who stands ultimately responsible for the formation of his most valuable collaborators.

It is also important to create a *committee for planning* and implementing, whose task it is to help the Bishop to set the topics to be considered each year in any of the areas of ongoing formation; to prepare the necessary aids; design the courses, sessions, meetings, and retreats; and organise the calendar properly so as to foresee the absences and replacements for priests. The expert advice of some specialists in specific fields may also be sought.

Whereas one group of directors is sufficient, various committees for planning and implementing the work can be established when needed.

---

[252] Cf. ECUMENICAL COUNCIL VATICAN II, Decree *Optatam Totius*, 22; CONGREGATION FOR CATHOLIC EDUCATION, *Ratio Fundmentalis Institutionis Sacerdotalis* (19th March 1985), 101.

91. Collaboration Between Churches

With regard to joint activities, by common agreement between various particular churches, whether on a national or regional level (through the respective Episcopal conferences), or principally between neighbouring or adjacent Dioceses, the organisation of different means of permanent formation and their specific contents can be set. Thus, for example, the interdiocesan structures such as schools and institutes of theology and pastoral care, entities or associations committed to the formation of priests can be utilised when suitable. Such combination of resources, aside from promoting an authentic communion between particular churches, may offer to all the most qualified and stimulating possibilities for ongoing formation.[253]

92. Collaboration with Academic and Spiritual Centres

Furthermore, institutes of study and research, centres of spirituality, like monasteries of exemplary observance, and shrines, constitute many reference points for theological and pastoral updating, oases of silence, prayer, sacramental confession and spiritual direction, healthy rest including physical relaxation, and moments of priestly fraternity. In this way also, the religious families may collaborate in the permanent formation of priests as well as contributing to the renewal of the clergy required by the new evangelisation of the Third Millennium.

Specific Needs of Certain Age Groups and Special Situations

93. The First Years of Priesthood

During the first years after Ordination, priests must be eager to find those conditions of life and ministry which permit them to put into practice those ideals learned during their formation period in the seminary.[254] These first years of priesthood, which make up a necessary confirmation of the initial formation following the first difficult contact with reality, are the most decisive for the future. These years, therefore, require a harmonious maturity in order to face difficult moments with faith and courage. For this reason, the young priests must benefit from a personal relationship with their own Bishop and with a wise spiritual father and from times of rest, of meditation and monthly recollection.

---

[253] Cf. JOHN PAUL II, Post-Synodal Apostolic Exhortation *Pastores dabo vobis* 79: *l.c.*, 796-798.

[254] Cf. *ibid*, 76: *l.c.*, 793-794

Keeping in mind what has already been said concerning the pastoral year, it is necessary to organise, in the first years of priesthood, annual meetings in which appropriate themes in theology, law, spirituality and culture are studied and dealt with in greater depth, as well as those special sessions dedicated to problems in morality, pastoral care and liturgy. Such meetings may also serve as occasions to renew the faculty of confession in the way it is established by the Code of Canon Law and by the Bishop.[255] It should be beneficial also that during these days, fraternity between the young priests and also with the more experienced ones be encouraged, allowing the exchange of experiences, greater friendship and the refined evangelical practice of fraternal correction.

Finally, it is essential for the young clergy to grow in a spiritual environment of genuine and refined fraternity, manifested in concern for one another, including their physical health and other material aspects of life.

94. After a Certain Number of Years

After a certain number of years of ministry, priests acquire a solid experience and the great merit of having spent all their efforts in extending the Kingdom of God through daily work. This group of priests constitutes a great spiritual and pastoral resource.

They need encouragement, genuine appreciation, a new deepening in all aspects of formation with the purpose of examining their actions, and a re-awakening of the motivation underlying the sacred ministry. They also need to reflect on: pastoral methods in the light of essentials, the communion among priests of the presbyterate, friendship with the Bishop, surmounting any sense of exhaustion, frustration and solitude and, finally, rediscovering the font of priestly spirituality.[256]

It is therefore important that these priests benefit from special and thorough sessions of formation in which, apart from pastoral and theological subjects, all other psychological and emotional difficulties that may arise in that period are examined. It is advisable that in such meetings, not only the Bishop take part, but also those experts who can give a sound and valid contribution to the solutions of the problems mentioned above.

---

[255] Cf. *C.I.C.*, cann 970-972.

[256] Cf. JOHN PAUL II, Post-Synodal Apostolic Exhortation *Pastores dabo vobis*, 77: *l.c.*, 794-795.

95. Advanced Age

The elderly priests or those advanced in years who merit special consideration, enter in the vital circle of ongoing formation, not so much regarding thorough study and discussion of cultural subjects, but rather "the calm and reassuring confirmation of the part which they are still called to play in the presbyterate".[257]

Besides the formation organised for the middle-aged priests, they can benefit appropriately from special periods and workshops to go deeper into the contemplative sense of the priest's life, in order to rediscover and love the doctrinal wealth of what they have already studied and to feel useful, as indeed they are. They can be involved in suitable ways in true and proper ministry especially as expert confessors and spiritual directors. In particular, they can share with others their own experiences, and encourage, welcome, listen and convey serenity to them. They can also be available whenever they are asked to "become effective teachers and mentors of other priests".[258]

96. Priests in Special Situations

Independently of age, priests may find themselves in "a condition of physical weakness or moral fatigue".[259] They contribute in an eminent way to the work of redemption offering their sufferings and giving "testimony by virtue of their union with the suffering Christ and with so many other brothers and sisters in the Church who are sharing in the Lord's Passion".[260]

For priests in these conditions ongoing formation must offer stimuli to "continue their service to the Church in a serene and vigorous way",[261] to be eloquent signs of the primacy of *being* over *acting*, of *content* over *technique*, and of *grace* over *exterior efficacy*. In this way they can live the experience of St Paul: "I now rejoice in my sufferings for you and fill up those things that are wanting of the sufferings of Christ, in my flesh, for his body, which is the Church" (*Col* 1:24).

The Bishop and his brothers must never fail to make periodic visits

---

[257] *Ibid.: l.c.,* 794.

[258] *Ibid.*

[259] *Ibid.*

[260] *Ibid.,* 41: *l.c.,* 727.

[261] *Ibid.,* 77: *l.c.,* 794.

to those brothers who are ill, who can be informed about events in the Diocese, in a way that makes them feel like active members of the clergy and of the Universal Church, which builds upon their sufferings.

Those priests close to concluding their days on earth spent in the service of God and for the salvation of their brothers, must be given particular and affectionate care.

The continual consolation of the faith and the prompt administration of the sacraments is followed by suffrages of the entire clergy.

97. Solitude of the Priests

The priest can experience a sense of solitude at any age and situation.[262] Far from understanding this as a psychological isolation, it could be altogether normal and a consequence of the sincere efforts to follow the gospel, and as such constitutes a valuable dimension of his own life. In some cases, however, it may be due to special difficulties such as alienation, misunderstandings, deviations, abandonment, imprudence, personal limitations of character as well as that of others, calumnies, humiliations, etc. He should not draw a bitter sense of frustration from it, which would be deleterious.

Nevertheless, even these moments of difficulties may become, with the help of the Lord, privileged occasions in which to grow on the road to sanctity and apostolate. In these occasions, in fact, the priest may discover that "there is a solitude filled with the presence of the Lord".[263] Obviously, this must not make the Bishop and the entire clergy forget the grave responsibility in avoiding every loneliness that stems out of negligence in the communion among priests.

Neither must he forget those brothers who have left the ministry, offering them necessary help, above all through prayer and penance. Proper charitable behaviour with them must not, however, lead them to consider entrusting them with ecclesiastical functions, which can create confusion and disconcertment, above all, on the part of the faithful, in view of their situation.

---

[262] Cf. *ibid.*, 74; *l.c.*, 791.

[263] *Ibid.*

CONCLUSION

The Master of the harvest, who calls and sends workers to work in his field (cf. *Mt* 9:38), has promised with eternal faithfulness: "I will give you shepherds after my own heart" (*Jr* 3:15). On this divine faithfulness that is always alive and operative in the Church,[264] rests the hope of receiving abundant and holy vocations to the priesthood. Moreover, it has already been proven in many countries that the Lord will not deny his Church the necessary light to confront the fascinating adventure of casting the nets into the sea.

The Church responds to the gift of God with acts of thanksgiving, fidelity, docility to the Spirit and a humble and persevering prayer.

In order to perform his apostolic mission, each priest will bear, engraved on his own heart, the words of the Lord: "Father, I have glorified you on earth, having accomplished the work which you have given me to do, to give eternal life to men" (*Jn* 17:2-4). For this, the priest will dedicate his own life to his brothers, living as a sign of supernatural charity, in obedience, in celibate chastity, with simplicity and with respect for discipline in the communion of the Church.

In his work of evangelisation the priest transcends the natural order to direct himself "in things that belong to God" (*Heb* 5:1). He, in fact, is called to raise man, generating in him divine life and making him grow towards fullness in Christ. For this reason, an authentic priest impelled by his fidelity to Christ and to the Church constitutes, in reality, an incomparable force of true progress for the entire world. "The new evangelisation needs new preachers and these are the priests who strive to live their priesthood as a specific way to sanctity".[265] God's works are performed by men of God!

Like Christ, the priest must present himself to the world as a model of supernatural life: "For I have given you an example, that as I have done to you, so you do also" (*Jn* 13:15).

The testimony reflected by his life gives the priest his qualification and constitutes his most convincing sermon. The same ecclesiastical discipline lived with real interior motivation turns out to be a providential aid in which

---

[264] Cf. *ibid.*, 82: *l.c.*, 800.

[265] *Ibid.* 82 *l.c.*, 801.

to live his own identity, foster charity and allow his testimony to shine forth. Without this, all cultural preparation or rigorous organisation would merely be an illusion. 'Doing' without 'being with Christ' is meaningless.

Here lies the horizon of the identity, life, ministry and permanent formation of the priest; a task of immense work: open, courageous, enlightened by faith, sustained in hope and rooted in charity.

In this urgent and necessary work, nobody is alone. It is necessary that priests be assisted by an exemplary, authoritative and vigorous action of pastoral government by their own Bishops, in communion with the Apostolic See as well as the fraternal collaboration of all the clergy and the entire People of God.

To Mary, Mother most faithful, each priest may entrust himself. In her who "was the model of that maternal love which must inspire all who co-operate in the regeneration of men in the apostolic mission of the Church",[266] priests will find constant protection and help for the renewal of their lives and help to draw out from their priesthood a renewed and more intense zeal for the extension of the Gospel on the threshold of the third millennium of Redemption.

His Holiness Pope John Paul II, on 31st January 1994, approved this Directory and authorised its publication.

JOSÉ T. Card. SANCHEZ
Prefect
✠ CRESCENZIO SEPE
Titular Archbishop of Grado
Secretary

---

[266] ECUMENICAL COUNCIL VATICAN II, Dogm. Const. *Lumen gentium* 65.

PRAYER
TO THE MOST BLESSED VIRGIN MARY

O Mary,
Mother of Jesus Christ
and Mother of priests,
accept this title which we bestow on you
to celebrate your motherhood
and to contemplate with you the Priesthood
of your Son and of your sons,
O Holy Mother of God.

Mother of Christ,
to the Messiah-Priest you gave a body of flesh
through the anointing of the Holy Spirit
for the salvation of the poor
and the contrite of heart,
guard priests in your heart and in the Church,
O Mother of the Saviour.

O Mother of Faith,
you accompanied the Son of Man
at the temple,
in fulfilment of the promises made to the Fathers,
give to the Father for his glory,
the priests of his Son,
O Ark of the Covenant.

O Mother of the Church,
among the disciples in the Cenacle
you prayed to the Spirit
for the new People and their Shepherds,
obtain for the Order of Presbyters
the full measure of gifts,
O Queen of the Apostles.

O Mother of Jesus Christ,
you were with him from the beginning of his life
and in his mission,
you sought the Master among the crowd,
you stood beside him
when he was lifted up from the earth,
consumed as the one eternal sacrifice,
and you had John, your son, close by,
accept from the beginning those
who have been called
protect their growth,
in their life ministry accompany
your sons,
O Mother of Priests.
Amen![267]

---

[267] JOHN PAUL II, Post-synodal Apostolic Exhortation *Pastores dabo vobis*, 82: *l.c.*, 803-804.